Richard Calvocoressi

MAGRITTE

PHAIDON

The author and publishers would like to thank the Centre Georges Pompidou, Paris, and all those museum authorities and private owners who have kindly allowed works in their possession to be reproduced.

The author wishes to thank David Sylvester and Elizabeth Cowling of the Menil Foundation, London, for their helpful suggestions.

Phaidon Press Limited, Littlegate House, St Ebbe's Street, Oxford
Published in the United States of America by E. P. Dutton, New York

First published 1979
© 1979 by Phaidon Press Limited
Reproductions © 1979 by ADAGP, Paris

ISBN 0 7148 1965 4
Library of Congress Catalog Card Number: 78-24732

Printed in Great Britain by Morrison & Gibb Ltd, London and Edinburgh

Magritte

Few people would deny that, of the many artists who participated in that full-scale readjustment of our sensibilities which called itself Surrealism, René Magritte remains today one of the most accessible. His paintings speak to us very directly. The great nineteenth-century French painter Gustave Courbet once said that he could not paint an angel because he had never seen one, and there is a sense in which this claim might also have been made by Magritte. (He actually admitted once that 'A woman's body floating above a city was an advantageous substitute for the angels that never presented themselves to my sight'.) Whilst other Surrealists painted angels, or more often devils, of their own invention, Magritte stuck closely to what he could see – the real world which we think we know but which, according to him, we do not know at all.

In many ways Surrealism was heir to the great nineteenth-century movements of Romanticism and Symbolism; it took the nineteenth-century protest against rationalism and materialism on to a different level but it was essentially the same protest. The Surrealists' search for the marvellous and their attempts to free the creative imagination from personal inhibition and social constraint were not new but they were given a new, twentieth-century emphasis and sense of urgency. And yet to explain Magritte's achievement simply in these terms is to misrepresent it. His position within the Surrealist movement as a whole was an ambiguous one. His relations with other members of the group, particularly André Breton, its high priest, were not always good. As an artist, he chose to ignore those esoteric phenomena which so excited his colleagues in Paris: neolithic and primitive art, the art of children and of the insane, medieval and symbolist painting, spiritualism, alchemical literature, psychoanalysis – none of these imaginative stimuli made much visible impact upon his painting. To look at a picture of the mid-1920s by Ernst or Miró is to be made aware of private fantasies at work, of rich and complex layers of meaning. Not so with Magritte. Any attempt to read his images as symbols of unconscious obsessions or repressed desires he firmly resisted. Although his early Surrealist paintings remind us strongly of the irrationalities of the dream world, a large proportion of his art appeals to our conscious mind. Magritte's statements about the world are often in the form of unanswerable questions or riddles, whose purpose may be to upset us but whose apparent logic we find it difficult to deny.

Magritte was not interested in accidental effects, automatism or other typically Surrealist techniques but, in his own words, in 'an objective representation of objects' – so objective, in fact, that his manner of representing them was deliberately prosaic. The Surrealists professed a common hatred of aestheticism and *belle peinture*, but it is in Magritte's cool, straightforward style, derived in part from his admiration for the paintings of the Italian Giorgio de Chirico (1888–1978) but also perhaps from his own work in advertising and publicity, that we find best exemplified this concern that the image should speak for itself, with as little interference from the artist as possible. Because they saw themselves as dealing with elemental experience – a kind of Jungian 'collective unconscious' – the Surrealists believed that their art would speak directly to a large audience, overriding cultural and aesthetic prejudice. By remaining aloof from the Surrealist preoccupation with the stream of consciousness, Magritte went further than his fellow artists towards realizing the ideal of a universal pictorial language – an ideal which in the final analysis is probably unattainable.

If in his art Magritte self-consciously set about to eliminate all traces of his personality, he certainly did not compensate for this in his life. Outwardly uneventful, it exhibited none of the noise and controversy which surrounded the activities of some of his Surrealist friends. Magritte preferred to live a life of bourgeois seclusion and anonymity. The romantic notion of the artist as outsider meant nothing to him: he was a man who painted pictures because he had to earn a living. He enjoyed listening to classical music (condemned by Breton for its formalism and inability to disrupt habitual modes of perception), liked reading, particularly detective novels and mystery stories (an enthusiasm he shared with some, but not all, of the Surrealists), but otherwise had few tastes or preferences (except for the cinema and, as we shall see, certain types of popular art). As far as we know he did not collect objects or artefacts. In both art and life he kept a low profile, eschewing the colourful and highly charged – an ostensibly dispassionate observer. 'Ostensibly', because Magritte's self-effacement was a mask which concealed an intensely subversive temperament, an urge to challenge our preconceived ideas about reality, to break our habits of thought and behaviour and force us into a new and heightened awareness of our surroundings. Underneath the harmless-looking uniform of bowler hat and dark suit, the artist prepares to administer a severe blow to our expectations. That kick in the groin, as it were, is made all the sharper by the bland, literal way in which Magritte's images are presented: his style, like his signature, gives nothing away. This paradox is of fundamental importance to the art of the Absurd, into which category Magritte can with justification be fitted: we have only to think, for example, of the deadpan way in which alarming but unexplained incidents or feelings are expressed in the work of Kafka, Ionesco and Pinter, or even in the films of Buster Keaton, which Magritte enjoyed watching.

Although Magritte's painting is sometimes described as 'veristic', it shares certain characteristics with the more explicitly 'poetic' kind of Surrealism: namely, a procedure by metaphor or analogy. In his book *What is Surrealism?*, first published in Brussels in 1934 with, significantly, a drawing from Magritte's *Rape* series adorning its cover, Breton claimed that Surrealism had done away with simile, with the word 'like': 'a tomato is a child's balloon'. Simultaneous or interchangeable images occur regularly in Magritte's paintings, coupled with a frequent use of dislocation – the removal of an object from its normal place or context and its introduction into an unfamiliar environment. Anatomical transpositions such as we find in *The Rape* (Plate 36) represent an extreme and brutal example of this practice, in which the ambiguity of the image reaches neurotic proportions.

The seemingly arbitrary combination of incongruous elements which was a popular device with the Surrealist painters stemmed from de Chirico, but the Surrealists were also in the habit of quoting a specific instance from one of their favourite authors, the Symbolist Isidore Ducasse (known as the Comte de Lautréamont), writer of nightmarish prose and verse: 'as beautiful as the chance encounter of a sewing-machine and an umbrella on a dissecting table'. The violence implicit in that image, together with its latent sexual content, epitomizes that *frisson* experienced by Breton when reading Symbolist and Decadent literature – a quality he called 'convulsive beauty' and which he recognized as being essential to the Surrealist image. Magritte spoke of his 'determination to make the most familiar objects scream aloud': the more familiar the object, the louder it would scream when divorced from its habitat, seen in a new light. The artist Marcel Duchamp had already shown how a manufactured object of daily use – bottlerack, comb, coat-hook – could assume a magical and sometimes threatening significance when raised to the level of a cult object or work of art; but his attitude to such standardized objects was supposedly one of complete aesthetic indifference, whereas Magritte's interest, as we shall see, was more positive. A glance at the formative years of his career (a word he would have disliked) reveals a quite different background from that of most other artists who became Surrealists.

Magritte was born at Lessines, in the Hainaut region of Belgium, on 21 November 1898. His brother Raymond was born in 1900 and their younger brother Paul two years afterwards in 1902. Paul Magritte turned out to be the musical member of the family; when he was eighteen he took piano lessons from E. L. T. Mesens. Mesens, a year younger than his pupil, was a remarkably versatile man who soon became one of René Magritte's closest friends. Poet, composer, Dada collagist and joker, he later worked as an art dealer and publisher. In 1923 he gave up music and a couple of years later, with Magritte and the poet Paul Nougé, formed the nucleus of the Belgian Surrealist movement – a movement which was always to keep a certain distance from the doctrinaire pronouncements of Breton in Paris, and which had a style and flavour unmistakably its own.

Magritte retained an interest in music throughout his life. One of his earliest surviving works (1920) is a portrait of a man playing the violin, and musical instruments, or decorative shapes connected with them such as scrolls or volutes, are common images in his paintings. More significant than this, however, is a group of collages executed in 1926, probably under Mesens's influence, while the two men were collaborating on the proto-Surrealist magazine *Marie*. These collages contain fragments of musical scores, many of them cut out to form a baluster, a recurrent motif in Magritte's paintings from 1926 onwards which has sometimes anthropomorphic, sometimes phallic connotations, and at other times is simply what it appears to be – an ordinary mass-produced object detached from its natural surroundings (in this case, a row of identical balusters). During the 1930s Magritte designed several sheet-music covers, including one for his brother Paul.

Magritte was never very forthcoming about his early life – we have to rely on one or two cryptic autobiographical sketches and the often imprecise reminiscences of friends and relations – and a degree of confusion surrounds his parents. We know that before her marriage Magritte's mother had worked as a milliner, but there is less certainty about the occupation of his father Léopold, who seems to have been some kind of manufacturer and trader in provisions. The family was comfortably off and moved around a good deal after Magritte's birth: from Lessines to Gilly, thence to Châtelet, Charleroi and back to Châtelet, before finally settling in Brussels in 1918. Part of Magritte's school holidays was spent with his grandmother and an aunt at the town of Soignies. It was there, whilst playing one day with a small girl in an abandoned cemetery, that he first became aware of painting as a special and somehow mysterious activity: 'We used to lift up the iron gates and go down into the underground vaults. Regaining the light again . . . I found, in the middle of some broken stone columns and heaped-up leaves, a painter who had come from the capital, and who seemed to me to be performing magic.'

The other crucial event of Magritte's childhood was the suicide of his neurasthenic mother, whose body was retrieved from the River Sambre on the morning of 12 March 1912. For many years it was thought that the face of the suicide had been found shrouded in her nightdress and that, when uncovered, it had worn an expression of calm beauty; it was also alleged that the thirteen-year-old Magritte had been present at the moment of discovery. Recent research has proved beyond doubt that such 'facts' form part of a legend probably fabricated by the Magritte family nurse. What matters is that Magritte was affected by the story of the nightdress: the image stuck in his unconscious and appears to have resurfaced in certain of his paintings where images of cover or concealment play a prominent role. Arguably the most sinister in this category are those paintings which depict the human head entirely swathed in fabric, such as *The Heart of the Matter* (Plate 19) and *The Lovers* (Plate 23). Magritte's ability to convey abnormal physical or psychological states – claustrophobia, anxiety, panic (for example, *The Hunters at the Edge of Night*, Plate 22) – is one of the most distinctive and original features of his art. Less immediately alarming but possibly also traceable to the fictive account of his childhood bereavement are the occasional references in his work to the serene composure of death, of which the several versions of *Memory* (Plate 41) are among the most haunting.

Magritte's first paintings, executed in a loose, impressionist manner, date from about 1915. The following year he enrolled as a student at the Académie des Beaux-Arts in Brussels. Disillusioned with the teaching there, his attendence over the next two years was sporadic. But he did make the acquaintance of Victor Servranckx (1897–1965), a fellow student whose interests and ideas were soon to exert a certain influence over the direction of his own art. Whilst at the Academy, or shortly after leaving it, Magritte was shown by his friend the painter and poet Pierre Bourgeois a catalogue containing reproductions of Futurist painting and for the next year or two he remained committed in his own work to echoing, probably not very satisfactorily, this radically new pictorial expression of the modern world. Unfortunately, very few of these so-called 'futurist' paintings survive, though we know from Magritte that they harboured strong erotic overtones. He associated this eroticism, which was to remain a conspicuous feature in his art, with the little girl in the cemetery and his original discovery of painting as a boy; he also described how it prevented him 'from falling into a more traditional search for formal perfection'.

Several works belonging to the years 1920–24, however, are characterized by just such a search, and it must have looked for a brief moment as if Magritte would become an abstract artist. The paintings of this period suggest a number of different sources within the tradition of Cubism and its cognates: the Orphism of Delaunay, with its dynamic fragmentation of solid matter through light and vivid colour contrasts; the more perfunctory, figurative Cubism of Metzinger; and Léger's great paintings of nudes in interiors of 1920–21. Magritte's *Woman* of 1923 (Plate 1) implies that his strongest debt was probably to Metzinger. The subject's featureless face and long body, the single viewpoint and bright lighting, and the artist's half-hearted attempts to 'analyse' the figure's solidity and merge it with its environment indicate that Magritte was not looking at a front-rank Cubist such as Picasso or Braque but at the distillation and popularization of their discoveries in the work of some of their followers. But whatever the prototype, Magritte brings to these early paintings a quality that is peculiarly his own. Nearly all depict female nudes, singly or in groups of three, as in many of Léger's figure compositions of this date, but there is an inescapable element of sensuality about them quite unlike Léger's monumental tubular women: the graceful curves of thigh and arm, the naturalistic colours including flesh pink and off-white, the relaxed poses, and the highlighting of sexual details such as the pubic hair – sometimes composed into the shape of a flower and at other times blurred as if the paint has been sprayed on with an airbrush (a piece of equipment with which, as a commercial artist, Magritte would have been familiar).

Magritte's retrospective opinion of such paintings was somewhat harsh. He considered them 'very evocative images but abstract and inert, and interesting, in the final analysis, only to the intelligence of the eye' – a judgement which ignores their inherent sensuality. Nor is there much in these canvases resembling the intricate geometry and narrow chromatic range of analytical Cubism: where abstract passages occur, they perform a decorative rather than a structural function. Nevertheless, certain works of this period seem inspired by the kind of pictorial idealism which we find in Léger's paintings of the 1920s. With this in mind we can now assess the part played by Victor Servranckx in Magritte's artistic development.

Magritte met up again with Servranckx when he went to work for a year under his supervision as draughtsman in a wallpaper factory, following his marriage to the twenty-one-year-old Georgette Berger on 28 June 1922. Magritte had known Georgette at Charleroi in his youth and had come across her again by chance in the spring of 1920, whilst out walking one day in the Botanical Gardens in Brussels. Before marrying, Magritte was obliged to perform his military service, which he did during the year 1921 and the first half of 1922 in an infantry regiment stationed first near Leopoldsburg and then at Antwerp. One of his companions was Pierre Bourgeois, brother of the architect Victor Bourgeois. Well before his conversion to Surrealism, Magritte was enjoying the company of avant-garde artists and writers in Brussels, where his pictures were occasionally exhibited and where he now settled with Georgette. But painting did not provide enough for the needs of the young couple and Magritte was forced to seek employment.

Servranckx, with whom he now found himself, was an abstract artist whose ideas coincided with those being voiced at the time by the magazine *L'Esprit Nouveau*, organ of the formalist movement known as Purism which had been launched in Paris after the 1914–18 War by the intellectual Amédée Ozenfant (1886–1966) and the architect Le Corbusier (1887–1967). Purism was essentially a reaction against the psychological upheaval of the War and against the iconoclastic side of Futurism, the nihilism of Dada and the idiosyncrasies which, it was felt, had been allowed to penetrate the Cubist revolution; it represented instead a 'return to order', to classical values of objectivity and harmony, combined with a twentieth-century belief in collectivism and anonymity. The Purists attempted to come to terms with modern industrial life in a positive, as opposed to a romantic or negative, fashion, and they held up the machine and the utilitarian objects which it manufactured as examples of the new beauty. Le Corbusier's ideal was *l'objet type* – the standardized, mass-produced object such as the bottle, carafe, bowl or glass which we use every day. Purism gave birth to an art, and more especially an architecture, of pure abstract shapes and mechanical precision.

Servranckx was certainly enthusiastic about such a programme; his own 'machine paintings' were much admired by the Purists. In collaboration with Magritte he now wrote an essay called 'Pure Art: in defence of the aesthetic', and there is in existence at least one picture by Magritte (of 1922) which points to his influence. In it a figure, abstracted but still readable as a stylishly dressed lady, is seen riding a horse watched by two more figures against a background architecture of geometrical or mechanical shapes, including some of those discs resembling traffic signs which recur in Servranckx's paintings of this period. The surfaces of the painting are smoothly finished in reds, greens and browns, giving an almost slick appearance, a quality not always absent from Servranckx's work. With Magritte, however, this smooth finish was to be turned to advantage in the surrealist paintings where it helps to throw into even sharper relief the unsettling nature of the image.

Of all the painters associated with Purism, it was Léger who contributed most to the movement's success. In his paintings of the 1920s, objects play an increasingly significant role; by 1927 such things as shells, leaves and keys have become enlarged and isolated, and seem to float in space before an abstract background. Léger's singling out of the object for special notice may be compared with a painting by Magritte of 1928 which has the revealing title of *Familiar Objects* (Plate 15). Here the head and upper torso of a man are seen from four different angles, one of which is repeated. In front of the eyes of each figure, in one case masking them completely, float banal objects: a sponge, a jug, a shell, a ribbon tied in a bow, and a lemon. But it is not only the objects which claim our attention: the figures are painted exactly as if they were objects too, sharing the same drab clothes, sober hairstyles and expressionless, impenetrable faces. This tendency to present man as a kind of *homme type*, standardized and anonymous-looking, is noticeable in several other works by Magritte. In *The Threatened Assassin* (Plate 8), for instance, three identical heads like a row of balusters peer in at the macabre scene from outside the window, while the two bowler-hatted 'detectives' waiting to trap the sex-murderer are in every respect twins, except that one brandishes a club shaped like a human limb and the other holds ready a net. (The figures outside looking in and the bowler-hatted men may both derive from two paintings by Max Ernst which were illustrated at the time in the periodical *La Révolution Surréaliste*.) The expression on their faces is equally passive and vacant. People in Magritte's paintings frequently stare like this in a distracted way, as if in a trance; others keep their eyes closed, as if asleep or dead.

The elevation of the manufactured object reaches a climax in Magritte's *The Betrayal of Images* of 1929 (Plate 30), which consists of a realistically painted briar pipe with the words *Ceci n'est pas une pipe* written underneath. Magritte's preoccupation with the division between image and language will be discussed later; here we need only recall that Le Corbusier illustrated just such a pipe on the final page of his book *Towards an Architecture*, first published in Paris in 1923 and a cardinal document of Purism. The twisted columns which separate the narrative in Uccello's disturbing masterpiece *The Profanation of the Host* have recently been proposed as a source for Magritte's frequent use of the baluster motif in his paintings. The Surrealists greatly admired Uccello and there is little doubt that Magritte looked at Old Master painting: in their symmetry, frontality and pronounced perspective, his composition often reminds us of fifteenth-century Italian painting. But a more likely source within the context which we have been examining is Léger's painting *The Baluster*, which hung in Le Corbusier's *Pavillon de l'Esprit Nouveau* at the 1925 Paris Exhibition.

If this account of Magritte's early development seems to have placed too much emphasis on his Purist connections, it is precisely because Purism and Surrealism were such radically opposed philosophies: the one rationalist and anti-individualist, the other romantic, with a taste for the eccentric and one-off. When Magritte became a Surrealist, his interest in the formal properties of ordinary objects was modified, as we shall see, by a new Nietzschean sense of their metaphysical reality beyond appearance which he inherited from de Chirico. However, the objects in his paintings bear no resemblance to the bizarre *objets trouvés* which other Surrealists were so fond of collecting.

After remaining for about a year in the wallpaper factory, Magritte left in 1923 to become a freelance poster and publicity designer. This activity continued until 1926 when he signed a contract with the Galerie le Centaure in Brussels, which enabled him to devote himself full-time to painting. There followed three years of intense artistic production in Paris, stimulated by contacts with the French Surrealists, but on his return to Brussels in the summer of 1930 Magritte was once again obliged to take up commercial work. His contract with Le Centaure had ended at the end of the previous year; shortly afterwards the gallery itself folded, with Mesens shrewdly, or bravely, buying up some two hundred of Magritte's canvases. Magritte's output of paintings declined considerably over the next six years as he channelled most of his energies into advertising. During this period he set up an agency called Studio Dongo with his brother Paul. It was not until 1937, with the increasing interest shown in his art by collectors like Claude Spaak and the Englishman Edward James, that his financial situation improved sufficiently for him to return to painting more or less full-time. Before assessing the effect which his various jobs in the commercial field had upon his art, we should first mention his discovery of the paintings of de Chirico, an experience which came as a revelation, turning him into a Surrealist almost overnight.

Probably during the year 1925, Magritte was shown by his friend the poet Marcel Lecomte some reproductions of de Chirico's work. He was particularly moved by *The Song of Love* (1913), in which an antique mask, a surgeon's red rubber glove and a green ball are juxtaposed in a severe Italian townscape of sharp perspectives and long shadows; in the background a train passes by behind a brick wall. The three displaced objects, entirely out of scale with their surroundings, assume a kind of monstrous prominence and life of their own. De Chirico was steeped in the writings of Nietzsche and Schopenhauer who, he believed, 'were the first to teach the deep significance of the senselessness of life, and to show how this senselessness could be transformed into art'. The hallucinatory intensity with which de Chirico focuses upon unrelated, commonplace objects, coupled with a psychologically disorientating use of heightened perspective and more than one viewpoint, suggests an undermining of apparent reality which induces a sense of alienation and which was to prove immensely attractive to the Surrealists.

Several of de Chirico's 'magic objects' find their way into Magritte's own paintings: the plaster hand (Plate 4); the ball (Plate 5); the dismembered limb (Plates 4 and 8); the antique marble head (Plate 41); and the train (Plate 40). In *The Difficult Crossing* (Plate 4), Magritte's use of the baluster, which here possesses an eye, is similar to de Chirico's use of the manikin figure in his paintings after 1914, where it replaces the statue as a mute human presence. The human-manikin analogy is central to Dada and Surrealist art and Magritte plays on the disturbing implications of this animate-inanimate inversion in a number of important works. In *Midnight Marriage* (Plate 10), a painting related to de Chirico's *The Two Sisters* (1915), the back view of a decapitated male head is juxtaposed with the hollowed-out face of a bewigged dressmaker's dummy. Magritte employs various dramatic methods for obscuring a person's face, including back views (Plates 6 and 39), wrapping the head in material (Plates 19 and 23), and concealing or replacing the head by an object (Plates 6, 7 and 15). There exists also a series of pictures in which a statue is shown in the process of metamorphosis into a female nude, or vice versa – it is deliberately not clear which. In the appropriately titled *Black Magic* (Plate 33), of which there are several versions, some kind of extraordinary transformation seems to be taking place before our eyes. Such works look forward to the paintings of petrified humans and objects executed in the early 1950s, of which *The Song of the Violet* (Plate 45) is one of the most memorable; or to the burlesques on Manet's *The Balcony* and David's *Madame Récamier* painted at about the same time, where the figures are replaced by wooden coffins.

Certain of Magritte's early Surrealist paintings (1926–7) are especially reminiscent of de Chirico in their general atmosphere. The crowded compositions and enclosed spaces, the recurrence of frames, windows, mirrors and 'pictures within pictures', the cold lighting and the occasional exaggerated perspective all help to recreate the enigmatic stage-set effect of de Chirico's 'metaphysical' interiors. But above all it is the pointlessness and absurdity of de Chirico's images which Magritte takes over and refines. *The Secret Player* (Plate 9), a large, impressive work painted in pallid colours which add to its unreal quality, is clearly intended to be read as dream imagery, in which the conventional elements of narrative, space and time, are surrendered to a series of dissociated events and impressions. To answer the question 'What does it mean?', we can only turn to other pictures by Magritte containing similar iconographic puzzles. The terrapin-like creature floating above the heads of the baseball players features in another work of this period, *The Robe of Adventure* (1926), a painting whose genesis was probably the suicide of Magritte's mother, and it foreshadows the sinister flying objects which we encounter in *The Black Flag* (Plate 31). The avenue of balusters sprouting blossom is a direct quotation from *The Lost Jockey* (1926), considered by Magritte to be his first successful Surrealist painting. The somnambulistic figure in the cupboard, masked and tightly corseted, is half nurse, half sex-object; no rational explanation of her presence seems possible, except that a strain of Sadeian sexual perversion or violence can be detected in several other paintings by Magritte (Plates 6, 8, 12, 21 and 36, and *Philosophy in the Boudoir*, 1947). Finally, the curtain drawn back to expose and frame the scene is a common theatrical device in works of this period.

There is an understandable temptation to interpret Magritte's early Surrealist pictures as a psychoanalyst would his patient's dreams – as voyages into the unconscious. Their titles – *The Magician's Accomplices, The Secret Player, Midnight Marriage* – hint at the enactment of shadowy private rites. In *The Reckless Sleeper* (Plate 11), the content of the sleeper's mysterious dream is represented almost ideographically by a few selected objects embedded in a molten substance. Dream motifs common to all of us are occasionally expressed in later paintings. The infantile sensation of growing infinitely large, for example, familiar to Alice in Wonderland and here transferred to an apple, is brilliantly evoked in *The Listening Room* (Plate 47). But on the whole Magritte's paintings after 1927 are less dreamlike, less complex in mood and organization, relying instead on the immediate impact of visual conceit or paradox – a strange meeting, an 'impossible' combination of objects, an even stranger metamorphosis. Many of them are analytical pictures, quasi-philosophical speculations into the nature and behaviour of things, or into the relationship between objects, the way we represent them, and the names we assign to them. Phenomena which we know to be reversals of natural law – a sky made of solid blue cubes, a wall of white clouds, an uninflammable object on fire, trees turned on their heads – seem feasible simply because Magritte has visualized them. With him, anything is possible: he acts like a conjuror, a magician, and it is no coincidence that he chose to portray himself thus, in *The Sorcerer* (Plate 43). In well-known works like *The Betrayal of Images* (Plate 30) and *The Human Condition* (Plate 34), he joins in the time-honoured debate about illusion and reality and asks fundamental questions about painting itself.

For this new kind of pictorial statement, both Magritte's experience of making collages and his activity as a commercial artist, soon to be resumed, proved to be of crucial importance. Max Ernst's collages of the early 1920s, which were among the first manifestations of visual Surrealism, gave Magritte the idea that painting too could be pieced together from disparate elements. Ernst's imagery, procured from traditional sources such as old engravings and illustrations to magazines, was synthesized in such a way as to provoke disruptions in narrative and scale, as well as curious changes in texture. Magritte quickly realized that this technique was ideal for the forcing together of separate realities, and although he made few collages himself, it has often been remarked how the principle of collage underlies all his painted work. His pictures are full of images of torn and splintered shapes: fragments of wooden floorboard and marble fireplace (Plate 7), a broken wall (Plate 10), a cut-out face (Plate 14), a pierced door (Plate 32). In *Titanic Days* (Plate 21), a picture which describes a sexual assault on a woman, the figure of the male attacker is contained within the outline of his struggling victim, as if superimposed; in other words, both the form and content of the image express the same violent physical union. This process of grafting or transplanting reaches an extreme in *The Rape* (Plate 36). Although both paintings are explicitly sexual in character, they are a far cry from the hot-blooded eroticism of, say, Picasso: the lighting remains harsh, the viewpoint cruelly frontal.

Whereas Max Ernst and the Cubists before him had incorporated in their canvases actual reminders of the physical world in the form of scraps of newsprint, pieces of wallpaper and so on, Magritte chose instead to render such things in paint with the precision and clarity of a *trompe-l'oeil*. There are numerous instances in his paintings where the surface texture of a particular material is simulated: wood, marble, granite, brick and stucco are the most common. Here again there is an affinity with Ernst, whose *frottages* are based on rubbings of similar textures. Like Ernst, Magritte appears to have undergone some kind of revelational experience whilst gazing, hypnotized, at the door-mouldings in a Brussels café in 1925.

As a wallpaper designer, Magritte would have been well versed in the techniques of illusionist painting. Most people are familiar with that species of wallpaper which comes in a variety of 'natural' finishes such as marble or wooden panelling, and there are plenty of occasions when Magritte reminds the viewer of this taste for *trompe-l'oeil* decoration, almost as if prompting him to ask 'Is it real or fake?' – a question which has little meaning within the context of painting. *Ceci n'est pas une pipe*: it is the image of a pipe which we see, not the thing itself. Magritte plays games of this kind in several important pictures. *On the Threshold of Liberty* (Plate 25), for example, shows a room 'papered' with images which we have met before in his work: jingle bells, fire, paper lattice-work, the façade of a house, trees, clouds, some grainy wooden planks, and the trunk of a nude woman. A note of menace is struck by the unexplained presence of a cannon aimed directly at the woman's body, which suggests that the confines of this mad cell will burst in an explosion of sexual violence. The 'picture within a picture' theme is common to several works of the late twenties; in *The Empty Mask* (Plate 27), written words instead of painted images stand in for the objects themselves. A painting related both iconographically and in its expectant atmosphere to *On the Threshold of Liberty* is *A Courtesan's Palace* (Plate 24); here the ubiquity of wood-grain adds to the intensely claustrophobic nature of the space. This feeling of enclosure is transmitted even when Magritte opens up his interiors to the sky outside, as in *Personal Values* (Plate 46), a later work which relies on simple reversals of scale for its disconcerting effect. By far the most striking use of simulated natural finish occurs in *Discovery* (Plate 18), where we see a woman's body undergoing one of those dramatic transmutations which are a speciality of Magritte. Metamorphic imagery causes much of the shock which we experience when looking at Surrealist art, nowhere more so than when a change of material, such as from flesh to wood, is involved. Meret Oppenheim's faintly repellent *Object (fur breakfast)* (1936), which consists of an ordinary cup, saucer and spoon, covered with animal fur, represents the ultimate in this genre of transmogrified things or beings.

Magritte's preference for isolating his imagery in separate boxes or compartments, and at times duplicating it, may also have had its roots in his commercial work. In *On the Threshold of Liberty* and similar paintings there is no serial or causal connection between the panels so that it is impossible to read the images as one would those of a strip cartoon, for instance. Duplicated images such as are found in *The End of Contemplation* (1927) and in the Tate Gallery's *Man Reading a Newspaper* (1927-8) may remind us of the pattern repeats on wallpaper or fabric, both of which Magritte designed. *The Double Secret* (Plate 14) and *Not to be Reproduced* (Plate 39) represent simple variations on this idea; in the latter work the effect is one of visual double-take. The parcelling up of the image assumes concrete form in *The Eternal Evidence* (Plate 29), which consists of five framed canvases, each like a small, self-contained icon and each showing part of a woman's body. Fitted together the parts do not add up to the whole – arms and shoulders, for example, are missing – so that the work resembles a weird party game or puzzle. Magritte's women (usually portraits of his wife Georgette) often have something of the mysterious and unattainable about them.

By dividing his pictures into sections, Magritte was able to schematize the Surrealist habit of conflating events or situations normally considered irreconcilable in the non-temporal art of painting: what is perceived, and what is remembered, imagined or dreamt. Instead of the shifts in focus and perspective of a de Chirico, something even more uncompromising happens: a break with the traditional notion of composition as a unifying aesthetic force. In *The Reckless Sleeper* (Plate 11) the entombed figure (the material world) and his dream (the mental world) claim equal attention as the picture's subject.

Between 1924 and 1927 Magritte did publicity work for the celebrated Brussels *couture* house Norine, founded by Norine and Paul-Gustave Van Hecke. In the thirties, Norine incorporated motifs from Surrealist paintings in some of their dress designs. Van Hecke was responsible in 1926 for bringing Magritte's painting to the notice of the Galerie le Centaure, which gave him his first one-man exhibition in the spring of the following year; among the sixty or so works on show were *The Signs of Evening* (Plate 5), *The Difficult Crossing* (Plate 4) and *The Threatened Assassin* (Plate 8). From 1928 to 1930 Van Hecke edited a little review called *Variétés*, to which Magritte contributed drawings, including a cover illustration based on his painting *The Lovers* (Plate 23). Magritte also illustrated catalogues for a Brussels furrier, which had mildly suggestive captions written by his friend Paul Nougé who became the main spokesman for Surrealism in Belgium. It would not be too fanciful to regard *The Rape* (Plate 36) as one of Magritte's fur illustrations given a nasty, ironic twist. The erotic ingredient in his early cubist canvases is even more pronounced in the fashion-plates which he designed for Norine and other firms, and in those which advertise mink coats draped provocatively round female models or manikins there is a noticeable tendency to throw into relief the soft texture of the fur. If in *The Rape* Magritte is suggesting an analogy between animal and human hair, he also brings to the surface a complex phobia – the same aversion to fur and feathers which Ernst plays on in many of his paintings. Magritte occasionally paints birds, both alive and dead, as in *Young Girl Eating a Bird* (Plate 12), a macabre work which is almost certainly symbolic of loss of sexual innocence.

To demonstrate how closely Magritte's painting and graphic design activities were interrelated during the early and middle years of the twenties one has only to look at a picture like the 1925 *Bather* (Plate 2). In many ways it is a transitional work. The colours are still the flat pastels favoured by the Purists, the 'architecture' is reduced to basic geometric forms, and yet an incipient Surrealism can be detected in certain details – the large ball in the background, the window revealing an expanse of sea, and the drapery at either side. It is instructive to compare this painting with a later work, *The Bather between Light and Darkness* (Plate 3), in which the same ideas are more successfully developed; here the ball has moved into the foreground, posing a real threat, the window looks more like a picture, and the reclining figure is naked, her eyes closed. But what concerns us about the earlier *Bather* is her stylish, Modiglianiesque pose, her Art Deco appearance, which scarcely distinguishes the picture from an advertisement for a woman's bathing costume and cap.

If Magritte's work in the commercial sphere provided him with a number of techniques and motifs which he found useful to his art, its most important legacy was perhaps a more fundamental belief in the functional character of painting – that painting is essentially a vehicle for an idea, not to be exploited for showing off sensuous colours or feats of technical virtuosity. Magritte deliberately affected a smooth, poster-like style, which is not to say that he was an inferior painter: anyone looking at the plates in this book will appreciate that he is in the presence of one who handles light and colour with rare skill. But on the whole the artist in Magritte's work is reduced to a neutral, recording role. This is fully consistent with one of the chief aims of Surrealism, which was to disrupt the senses by inverting traditional modes of communication, whether written, spoken or visual: the more conventional the language, the greater the derangement. The photographs which Magritte took as 'notes' towards some of his paintings, for which his wife and friends would pose, disclose even more clearly his indifference to the medium. (They also show how childish at times his sense of humour could be, but how often this childishness concealed a sharp cutting edge.)

Magritte claimed, somewhat over-ingenuously, that he had no tastes in art, his admiration being reserved, rather like Léger's was, for the largely unsigned products of popular culture: postcards, shop signs, gangster and suspense films, illustrations to thriller magazines. It has often been pointed out how this liking for ephemera is mirrored in his paintings, and David Sylvester has recently discovered a source in erotic postcards for a handful of works. (Erotic or pornographic postcards were collected by other Surrealists, notably Dali and the poet Paul Eluard.) There can be no question that a certain genre of French and German picture postcards of the 1900–1920 period greatly appealed to Magritte's Surrealist eye. There was, for example, a wealth of cards on the theme of travel in which, by a primitive photo-montage technique, objects and animals were shown flying about the sky in defiance of gravity – cars, turtles, fish, and even a lion – as well as legitimate flying vehicles such as Zeppelins, airships, bi- and tri-planes and balloons. The attraction for Magritte of this surprisingly rich vein of fantasy becomes perfectly clear if we consider *The Black Flag* (Plate 31), *The Age of Enlightenment* (Plate 48) or a number of similar paintings. But it should not be forgotten that some of the more grotesque allegorical paintings of the Flemish Old Masters contain bizarre flying creatures. Bosch and Bruegel, both greatly admired by the Surrealists, are the most obvious examples, but the works of Huys and Lucas van Leyden also boast monstrous inventions such as reappear in Magritte: severed limbs treated as independent beings (*Intermission*, Plate 16), deformed or elongated noses (*The Philosopher's Lamp*, 1936), and various kinds of hybrid. Magritte could have seen works by these artists in the museum in Brussels. He might also have found in early Flemish religious painting a precedent both for his suspension in space of dislocated parts of the face and body, as in *The Age of Enlightenment*, and for the incorporation of written words in the composition.

During the three years which he spent in Paris (1927–30), Magritte produced a number of works which were probably influenced by his proximity to certain of the Paris-based Surrealists. He had already been impressed by Max Ernst's basically figurative paintings of the early twenties, some of which were illustrated in the magazine *La Révolution Surréaliste*, but he was now drawn to the more informal, abstract configurations in the work of artists like Arp, Miró and, to a lesser extent, Ernst himself. These paintings of Magritte's are characterized by the emergence of biomorphic or organic shapes, as in *Intermission* (Plate 16) and *The Celestial Muscles* (Plate 17) – the latter bears a slight formal resemblance to Ernst's forest paintings – and by a curious device of setting images in a substance which is sometimes soft and malleable and which at other times looks like one of Arp's painted wooden reliefs (Plates 11 and 28). The pages of *La Révolution Surréaliste* were sprinkled with articles and photographs exploring such typically Surrealist interests as hypnosis, madness and hysteria, and there are a handful of paintings by Magritte which reflect these tastes (Plates 13 and 20). On the whole Magritte was much less enthusiastic than his Parisian friends were about such subjects, though he did contribute a drawing to the book which the Surrealists produced in 1933 as a homage to the murderess Violette Nozière.

The Paris period is important primarily for Magritte's introduction of words into his pictures. The relationship between an object, its name and its representation was discussed by Magritte at the time in an illustrated text which he published in *La Révolution Surréaliste*. This relationship is examined in a series of paintings in which words start by designating images of the material world, proceed to challenge them, and end up by replacing them altogether, so that the effect is not unlike that of a work of conceptual art (*The Empty Mask*, Plate 27). In his text 'Words and Images', Magritte wrote that 'a nondescript form can replace the image of an object', an idea which lies behind *The Use of Speech* (Plate 26). In shape and colour the nondescript forms in this painting, marked 'mirror' and 'woman's body', strongly resemble excrement, but in another work, *The Magic Mirror* (Plate 28), there is a closer affinity between the partly flesh-pink biomorph and its written designation, 'human body'. The notion of painting as a sign language was dear to the Surrealists, but Magritte's use of words is quite different from, say, the visual shorthand practised by Miró, however much at times it seems to parody it. Not without reason have his paintings been compared to the picture language of children's alphabet books.

In the 1930s Magritte's conception of his own painting changed. Instead of bringing about a collision between incompatible things, he saw it as solving certain hypothetical problems: 'the problem of the door' (Plate 32), 'the problem of the window' (Plate 34), 'the problem of shoes' (Plate 37), and so on. We should think of these works as pictorial arguments in which the various stages of the argument have become inextricably fused, according to a principle of affinity between objects which Magritte recognized. The version of *The Red Model* illustrated here was one of a handful of works painted specially for Edward James, an enthusiastic collector of Surrealist art who invited Magritte to stay with him in London early in 1937. This visit was engineered by E. L. T. Mesens who had been one of the organizers of the International Surrealist Exhibition in London the previous year and who later took over the running of the London Gallery, where Magritte was given a one-man show in 1938. *The Red Model* exists in at least three versions; the James variant, which is the last, is the largest and most elaborate (and, as such, possibly the least powerful in impact). Lying in the shingle beneath Magritte's extraordinary metamorphic creation (boot or foot? container or thing contained?), which here has none of the fetishistic overtones suggested by the woman's high-heeled shoes in the Sadeian *Philosophy in the Boudoir* (1947), one can make out some English coins, the stub of a cigarette, a match, and a crumpled fragment of newspaper – emblems of transience, perhaps, in a modern *Vanitas* still-life. On closer inspection the piece of newspaper is seen to contain a reference to Magritte's own work in the form of a reversed photograph of an earlier painting, *Titanic Days* (Plate 21), whose subject is a sexual attack on a woman. Another painting commissioned by James, *Not to be Reproduced* (Plate 39), which is an ironic portrait of the collector, can also be interpreted as a kind of oblique self-portrait. The clue here is the book on the mantelpiece, *The Adventures of Arthur Gordon Pym* by Edgar Allan Poe, which, unlike James, is faithfully reflected in the mirror. Poe was Magritte's favourite author; he borrowed several titles for his paintings from works by Poe. (Magritte's titles are usually allusive or punning rather than descriptive; occasionally they deliberately contradict the image.)

Given the worsening political situation in Europe during the thirties, it is not surprising that Magritte, like so many artists and writers of his generation, should have briefly belonged to the Communist Party. But politics had little effect on his painting. A possible exception is *The Black Flag* (Plate 31), which may refer to an event such as the bombing of Guernica during the Spanish Civil War, and whose title has a decidedly anarchist ring. (There may also be an ironic sideways glance at the Belgian Communist Party, whose newspaper was called *The Red Flag*.) What did affect Magritte, however, was the experience of living out the Second World War in occupied Belgium, which persuaded him to alter radically his attitude towards his own painting and towards Surrealism in general. In 1943 he began to paint in a bright, colourful style which parodied the Impressionist paintings of Monet and Renoir, thus making use of an established and popular idiom for his own unpredictable ends. This 'radiant period', as it was dubbed, lasted for about four years; it is characterized by paintings in which pleasurable or erotic sensations are substituted for the feeling of anxiety generated by the pre-war Surrealist works – sometimes irreverently so, as in *The Ocean* (Plate 42).

In 1946 Magritte broke with Breton over these 'impressionist' pictures. In a letter to Breton of 24 June of that year he renounced Surrealism in the following terms:

> This sense of chaos, of panic, which Surrealism hoped to foster so that everything might be called into question was achieved much more successfully by those idiots the Nazis, and then there was no getting away from it. I painted a picture, *The Black Flag*, which gave a foretaste of the terror which would come from air missiles, and I'm not proud of it . . . Against widespread pessimism, I now propose a search for joy and pleasure.

This was followed a few months later by the publication of a manifesto, *Surrealism in Full Sunlight*, signed by Magritte and several other Belgian Surrealists. But the public was not to be let off so lightly. The following year (1947) Magritte tried a little experiment. To counteract the complacency, the false sense of optimism, which he thought might have resulted from the impressionist works, he painted in a short space of time a number of deliberately grotesque subjects in a savage, impetuous manner. He called these paintings by a vulgar French word, *vache*. In *The Pebble* (Plate 44), however, Magritte shows how beautifully he could paint a shocking subject if he so wished.

The *vache* interlude was a brief and unpopular one and Magritte soon retreated into his old style. Much of the sting, however, had gone out of his work: there is something flat, even a little trite, about the imagery of many of the paintings executed in the 1950s and '60s. This was the period when, for mainly commercial reasons, Magritte was forced to paint variations of his own previous work, and while it is true to say that he constantly guarded against the danger of mechanical repetition, the several versions that exist of a particular painting seldom add to what we already know. Seen in quantity, the later works tend towards monotony. In a sense he had nothing new to say after completing in 1953 a large decorative scheme for the Casino at Knokke-le-Zoute, which he called *The Enchanted Domain*. This frieze, with its quotations from earlier paintings, can be taken as a compendium of his art, a final summing up of the ideas which had engaged his mind for thirty years.

In the sixties, public interest in Magritte increased enormously and there were two major retrospective exhibitions of his work before his death in the summer of 1967. This rediscovery of a by then almost neglected figure was largely due to the enthusiasm of certain questioning young artists, mostly American, who realized that Magritte had anticipated and attempted to come to grips with many of the issues which concerned them. His background in commercial art, his interest in mass culture and use of multiplied imagery, his belief that art is as much the product of intellectual activity as of instinct or perception, and his demystification of the artist's status to that of an objective recorder of information: all this profoundly influenced a generation of artists who are still with us today.

Select Bibliography

Waldberg, Patrick, *René Magritte*. Brussels, 1965.
Soby, James Thrall, *René Magritte*. Museum of Modern Art, New York, 1965.
Gablik, Suzi, *Magritte*. London, 1970.
Passeron, René, *René Magritte*. Paris, 1970.
Scutenaire, Louis, *Avec Magritte*. Brussels, 1977.
Torczyner, Harry, *Magritte: Ideas and Images*. New York, 1977.

EXHIBITION CATALOGUES

René Magritte: le mystère de la réalité. Museum Boymans - van Beuningen, Rotterdam, 1967 (introduction by Jean Dypréau).
Sylvester, David, *Magritte*. Arts Council of Great Britain, Tate Gallery, London, 1969.
Ades, Dawn, and others, *Dada and Surrealism Reviewed*. Arts Council of Great Britain, Hayward Gallery, London, 1978 (especially sections 9, 13, 16 and 17).
Rétrospective Magritte. Palais des Beaux-Arts, Brussels, and Centre Georges Pompidou, Paris, 1978–9.

A full bibliography up to 1965, compiled by André Blavier, is provided at the back of Waldberg.

Outline Biography

1898	Born 21 November at Lessines, in the province of Hainaut, Belgium, the eldest of three brothers.
1912	Suicide of Magritte's mother.
1915	Begins to paint, in an impressionist style.
1916–18	Studies intermittently at the Académie des Beaux-Arts in Brussels, where his family settles in 1918.
1919	Paintings influenced by Futurism.
1920	Meets E. L. T. Mesens.
1921–22	Military Service.
1922	Marries Georgette Berger. Works for a year in a wallpaper factory.
1923	Becomes poster and publicity designer. Paintings of this period owe much to Magritte's interest in Cubism and Purism.
1925	Collaborates with Mesens on Dada review *Œsophage*. Encounters work of de Chirico.
1926	Collaborates with Mesens on review *Marie*. Executes collages. First Surrealist paintings.
1927	First one-man exhibition, in Brussels. Moves to Le Perreux-sur-Marne, a Paris suburb.
1927–30	In close touch with Parisian Surrealists, with whom he exhibits. Maintains contact with Belgian Surrealists.
1929	Magritte's text 'Words and Images' published in *La Révolution Surréaliste*, 15 December. Termination of contract with Brussels dealer.
1930	Returns to Brussels. Obliged to work again as a commercial artist. Sets up advertising agency with his brother Paul.
1936	First exhibition of Magritte in U.S.A. Takes part in the International Surrealist Exhibition in London.
1937	At the invitation of Edward James, spends several weeks in London.
1938	Takes part in the International Surrealist Exhibition, Paris. One-man exhibition in London.
1940	Leaves Belgium before the German invasion and spends three months at Carcassonne in the south of France. Returns to Brussels.
1943–47	Impressionist period.
1947–48	*Vache* period.
1953	Executes large decorative project, called *The Enchanted Domain*, for the Casino at Knokke-le-Zoute, Belgium.
1954	First retrospective exhibition, Brussels.
1965	Retrospective exhibition, New York.
1967	Retrospective exhibition, Rotterdam. Death of René Magritte in Brussels, 15 August.

List of Plates

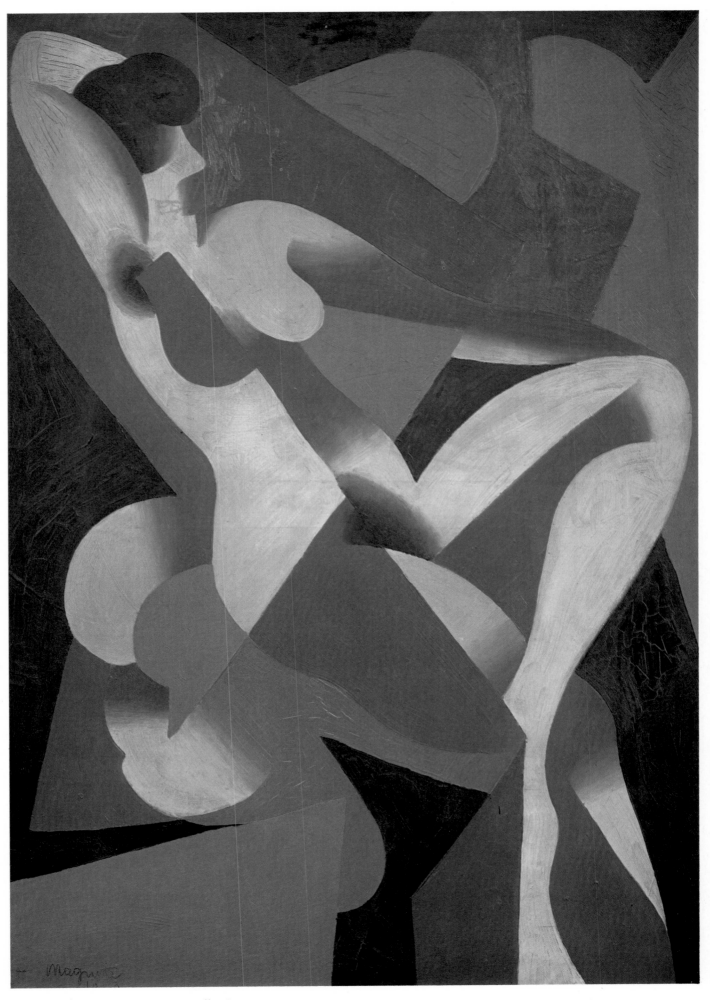

1. *Woman/Femme*. 1923. Private collection

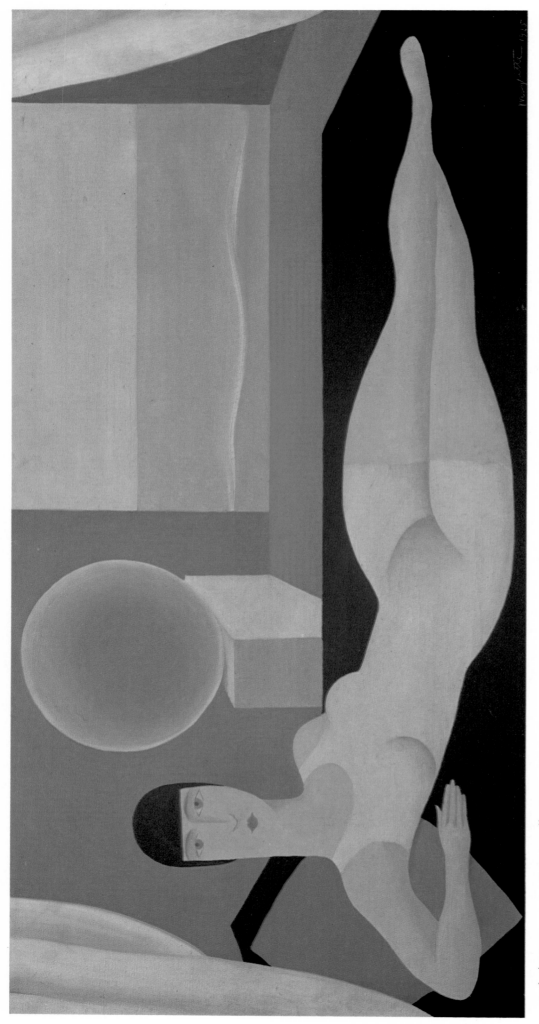

2. *Bather/Baigneuse*. 1925. Private collection

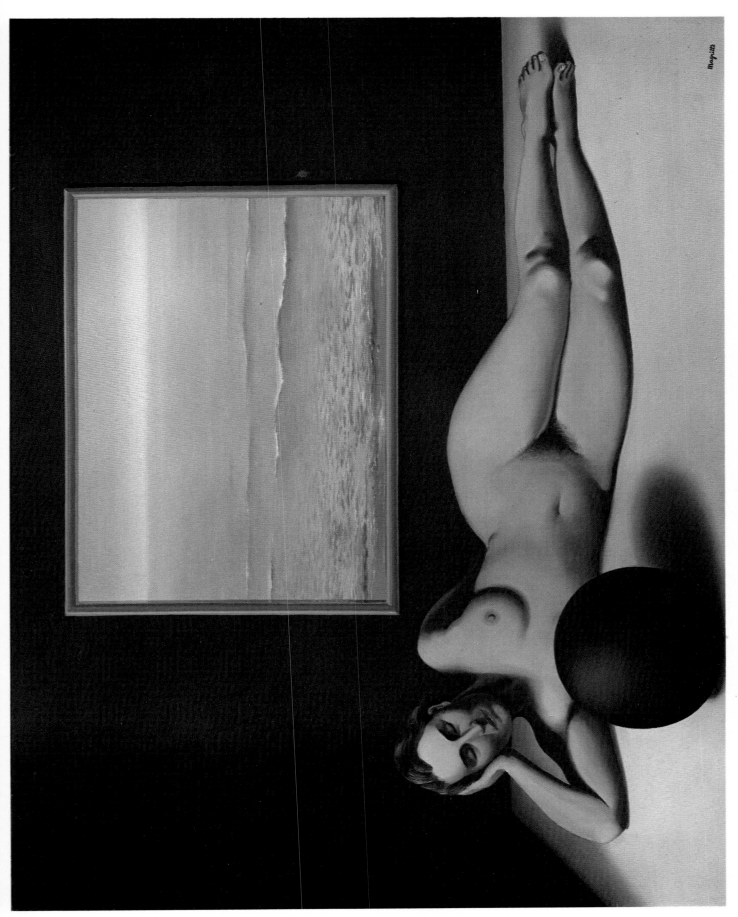

3. *The Bather between Light and Darkness/La baigneuse du clair au sombre.* 1935 or 1936. Private collection

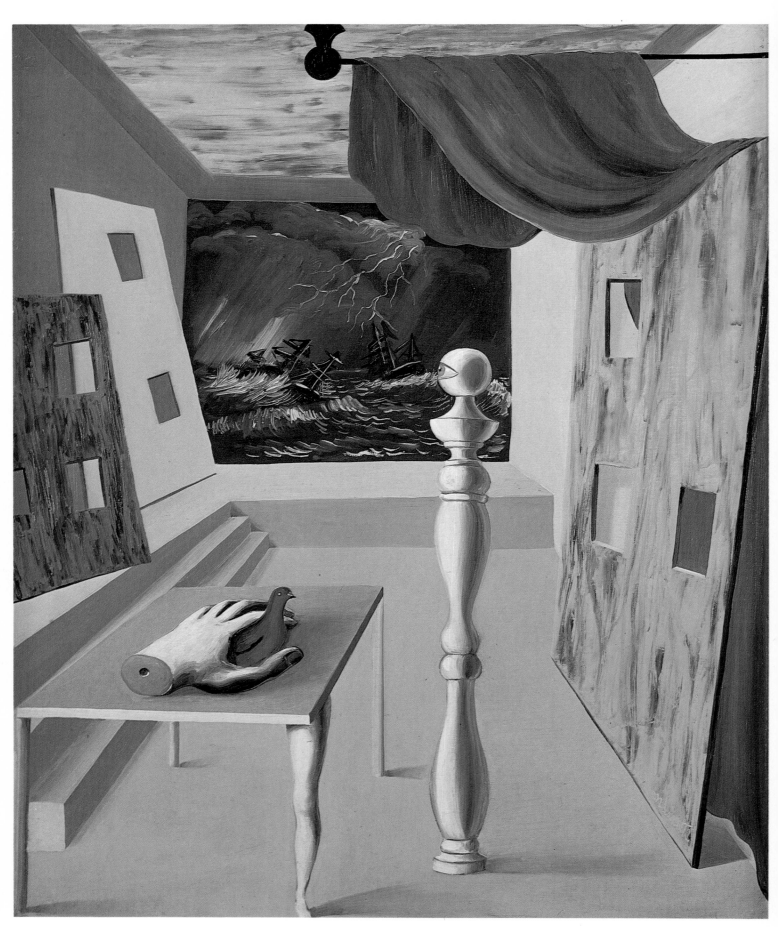

4. *The Difficult Crossing/La traversée difficile*. 1926. Private collection

5. *The Signs of Evening/Les signes du soir.* 1926. Private collection

6. *The Magician's Accomplices/Les complices du magicien.* 1926. Private collection

7. *The Man of the Sea/L'homme du large.* 1926 or 1927. Brussels, Musées royaux des Beaux-Arts de Belgique

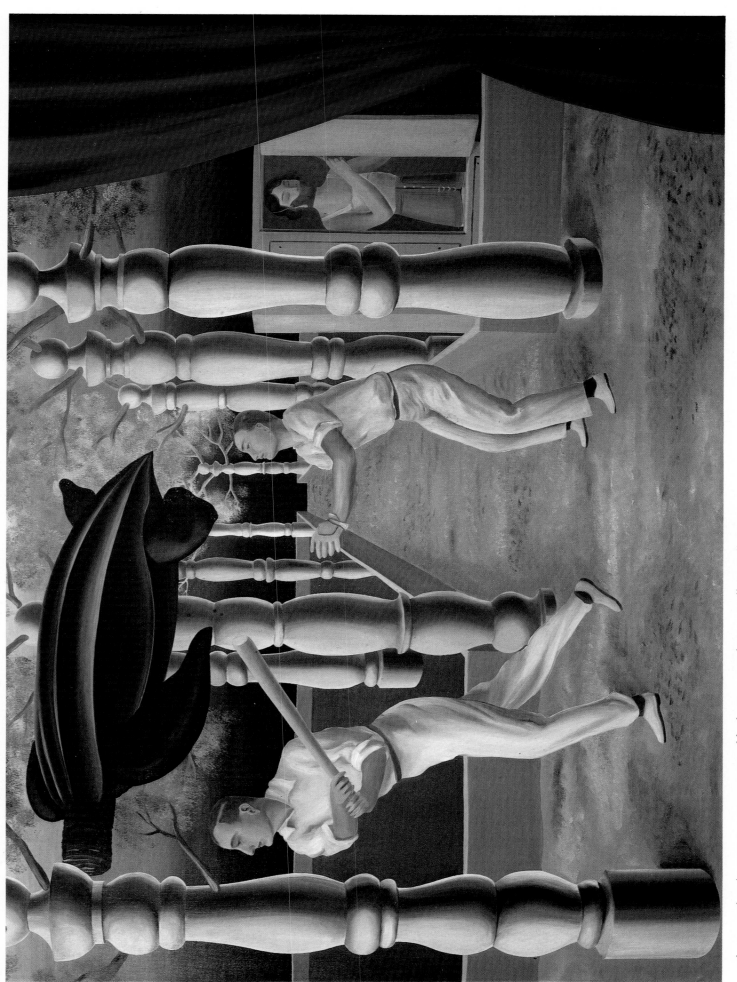

9. *The Secret Player/Le joueur secret*, 1927. Knokke-le-Zoute, Belgium, Nellens Collection

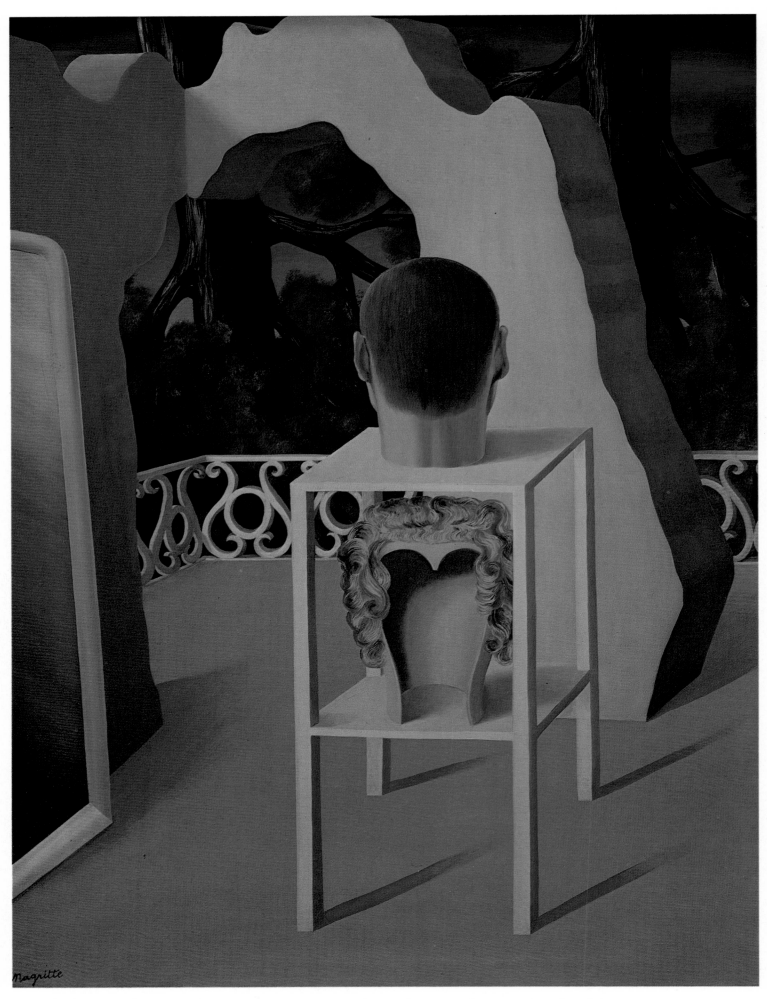

10. *Midnight Marriage/Le mariage de minuit.* 1926 or 1927. Brussels, Musées royaux des Beaux-Arts de Belgique

11. *The Reckless Sleeper/Le dormeur téméraire*. 1927. London, Tate Gallery

12. *Young Girl Eating a Bird/Jeune fille mangeant un oiseau.* 1927. Düsseldorf, Kunstsammlung Nordrhein-Westfalen

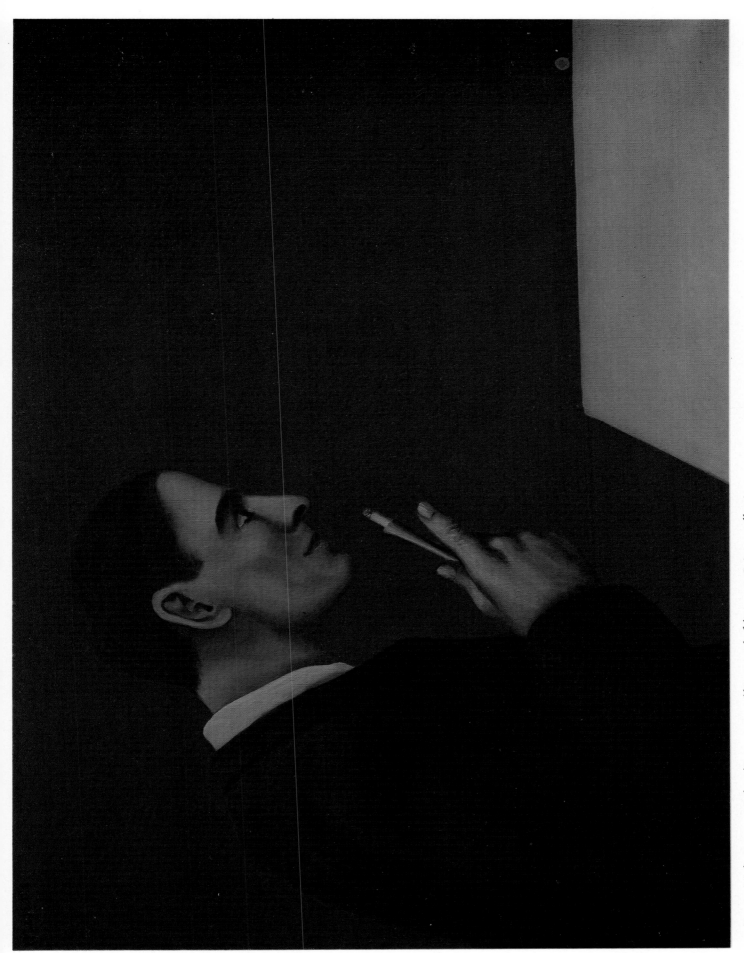

13. *Person Meditating on Madness/Personnage méditant sur la folie.* 1928. Private collection

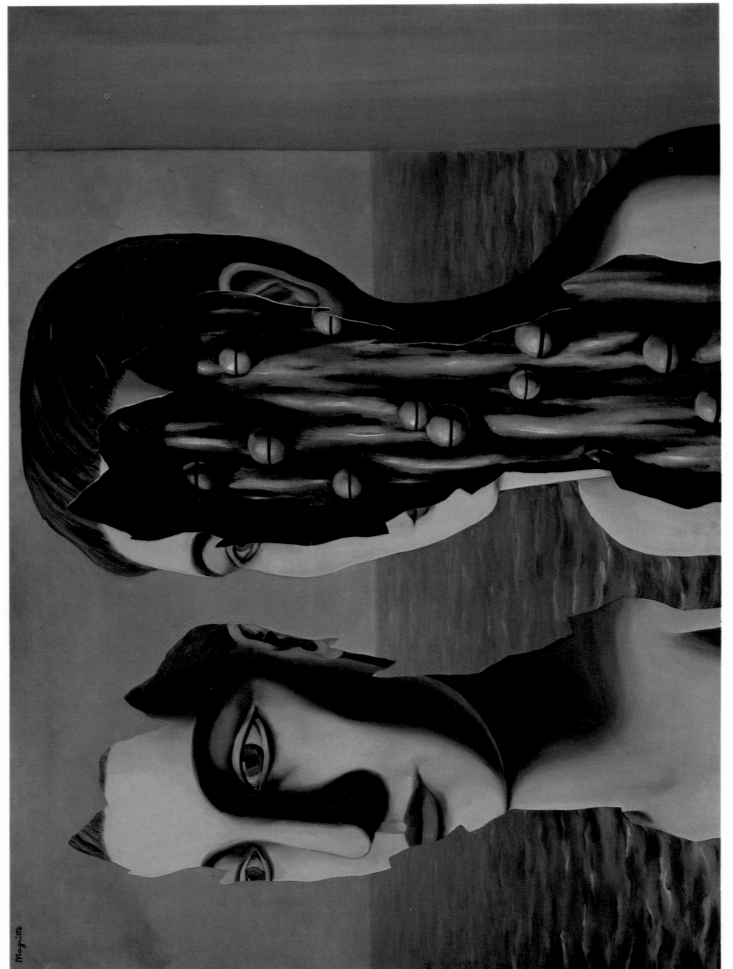

14. *The Double Secret/Le double secret.* 1927. Belgium, private collection

15. *Familiar Objects/Les objets familiers.* 1928. Private collection

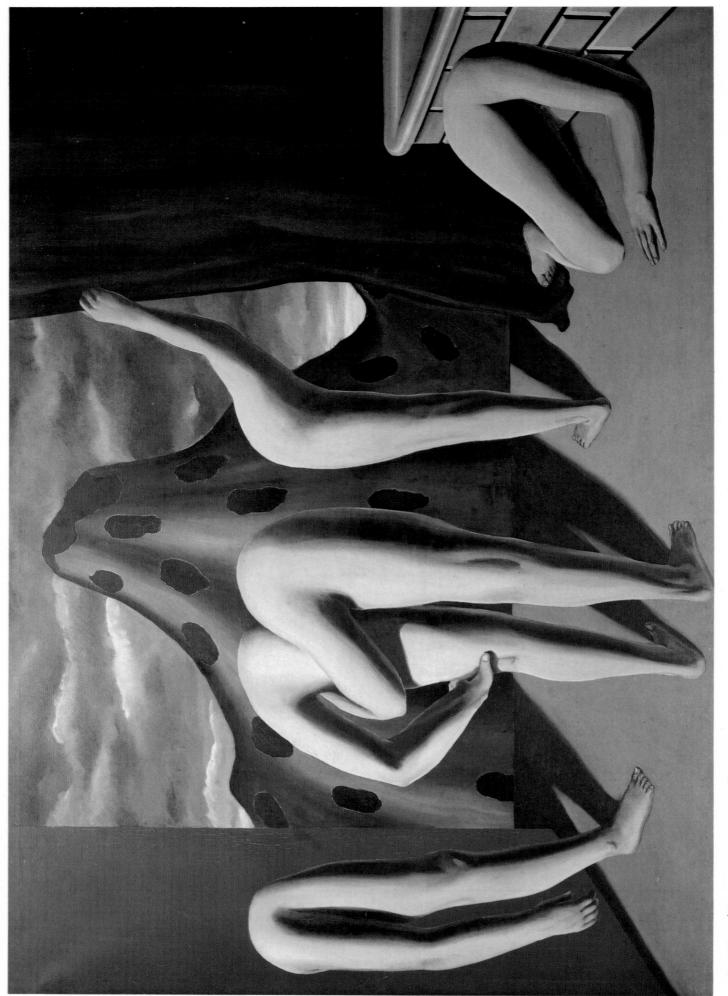

16. *Intermission/Entracte.* 1927. Private collection.

17. *The Celestial Muscles/Les muscles célestes.* 1927. Private collection

18. *Discovery/Découverte*. 1927. Private collection

19. *The Heart of the Matter/L'histoire centrale.* 1928. Rhode-St-Genèse, Belgium, Marcel Mabille Collection

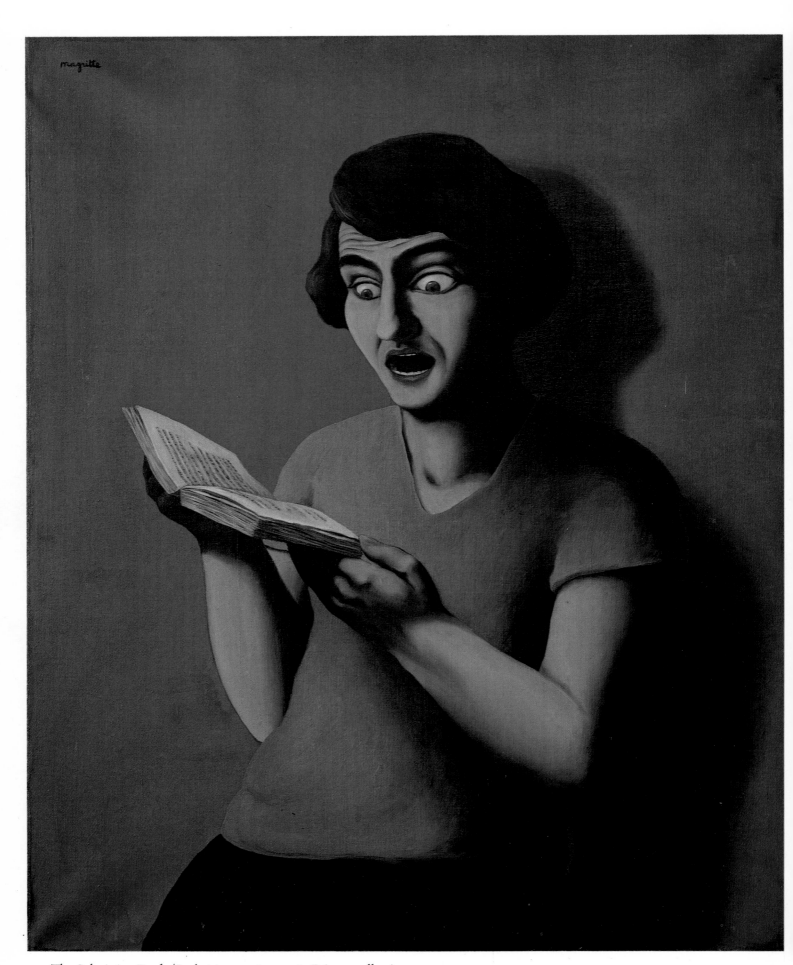

20. *The Submissive Reader/La lectrice soumise.* 1928. Private collection

21. *Titanic Days/Les jours gigantesques.* 1928. Private collection

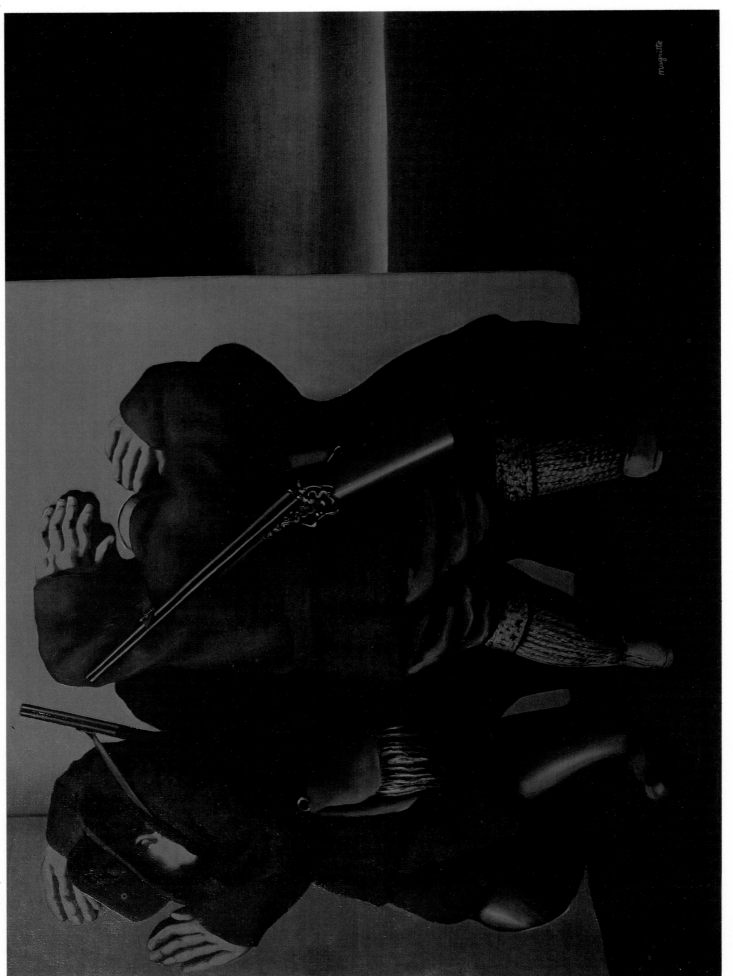

22. *The Hunters at the Edge of Night/Les chasseurs au bord de la nuit*. 1928. Private collection

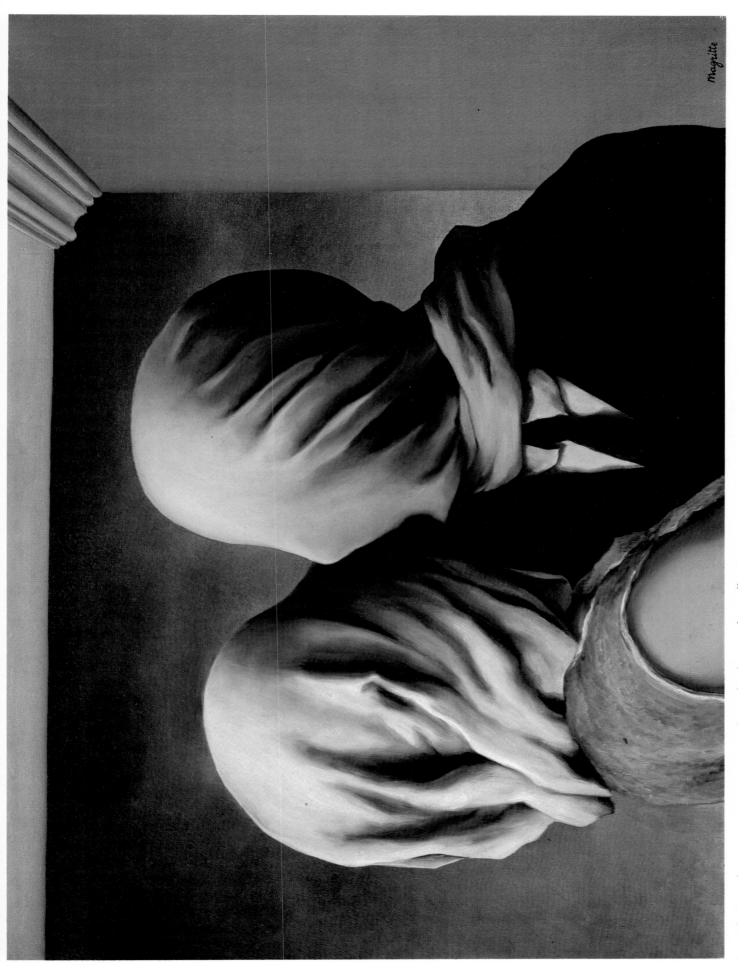

23. *The Lovers/Les amants.* 1928. New York, Richard S. Zeisler Collection

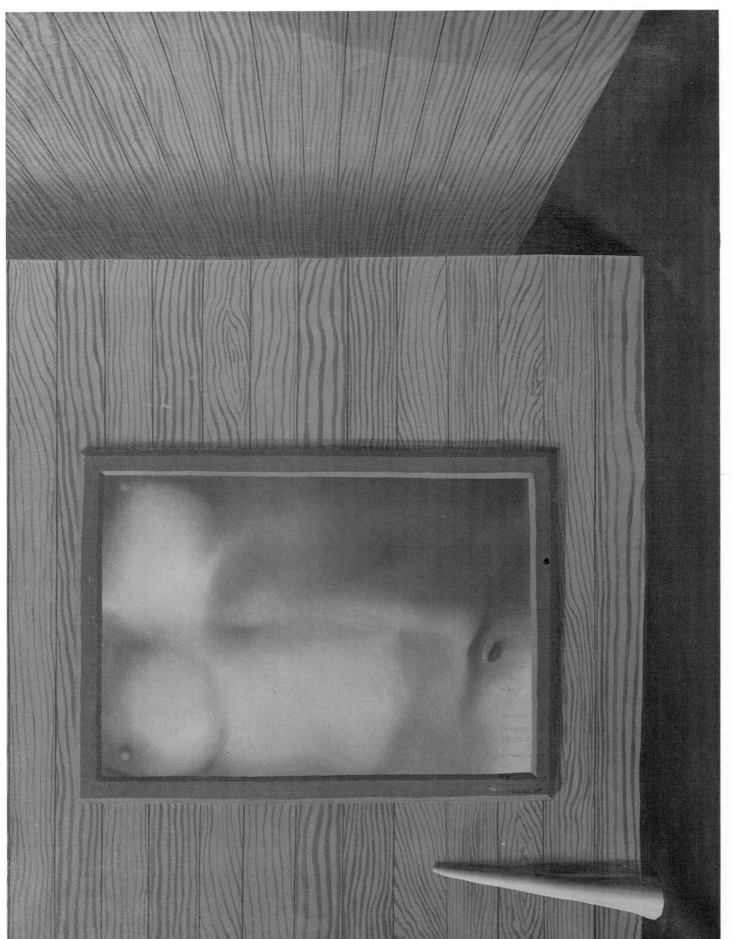

24. *A Courtesan's Palace/Le palais d'une courtisane.* 1928. Private collection

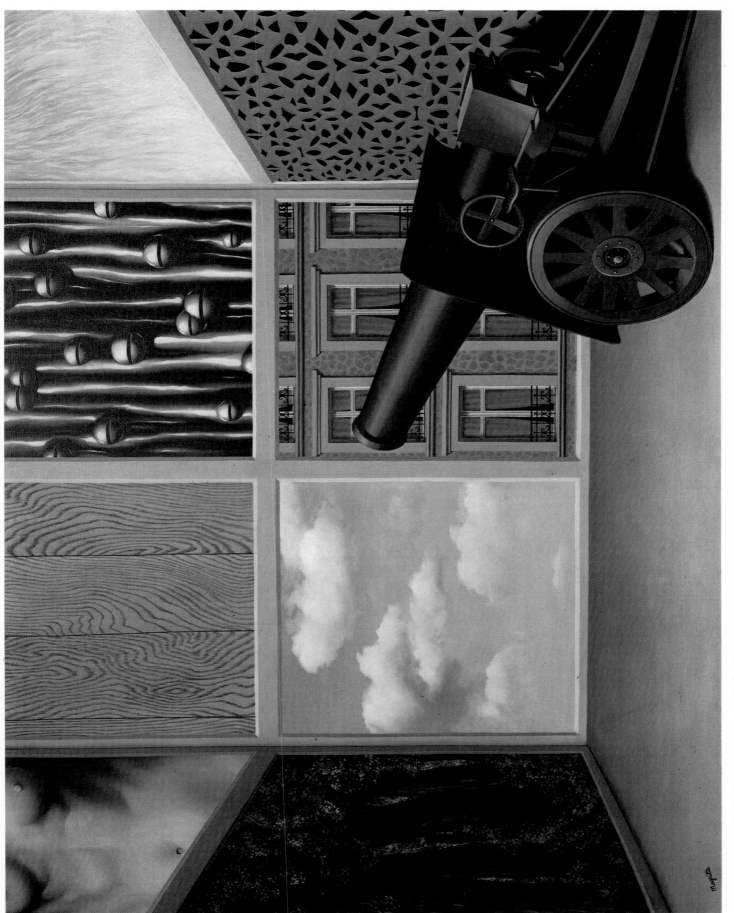

25. *On the Threshold of Liberty/Au seuil de la liberté.* 1930. Rotterdam, Museum Boymans - van Beuningen

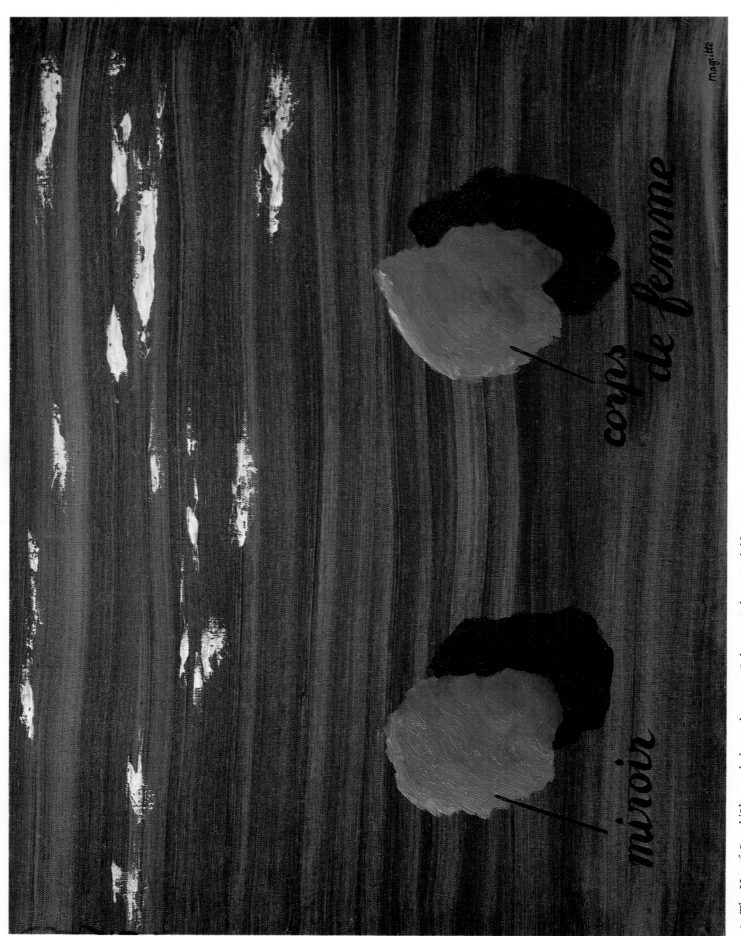

26. *The Use of Speech/L'usage de la parole.* 1928. Cologne, Galerie Rudolf Zwirner

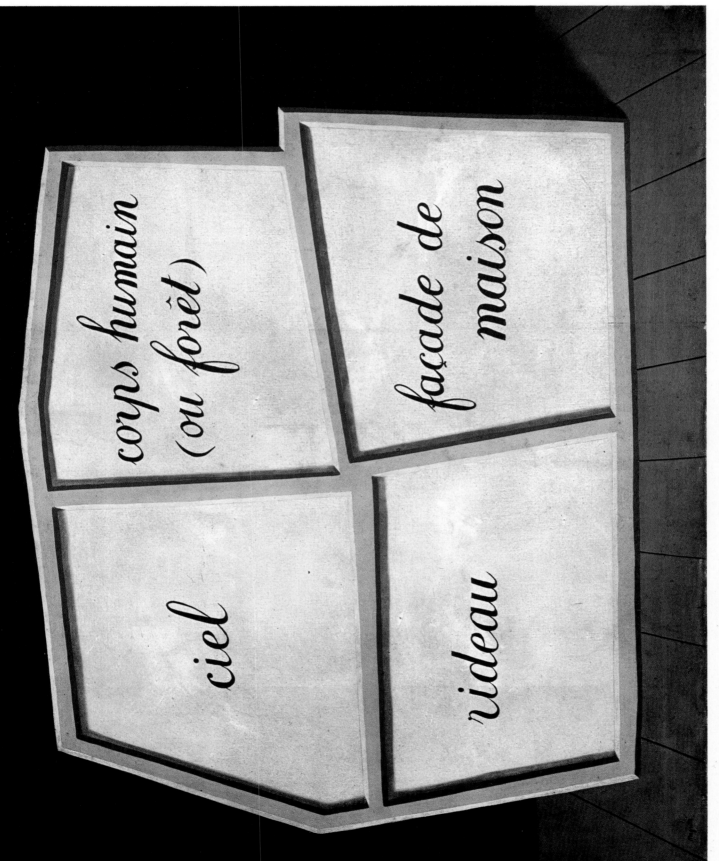

27. *The Empty Mask*/*Le masque vide*. 1928. Düsseldorf, Kunstsammlung Nordrhein-Westfalen

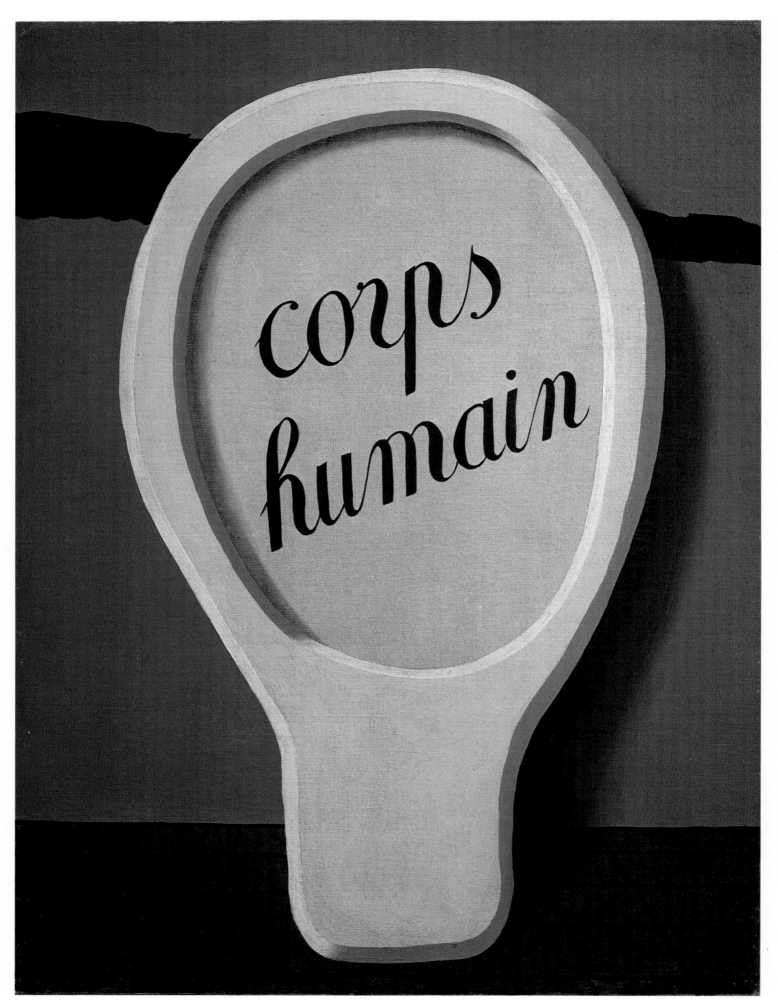

28. *The Magic Mirror/Le miroir magique.* 1929. Private collection

29. *The Eternal Evidence/L'évidence éternelle.* 1930. Houston, Menil Foundation Collection

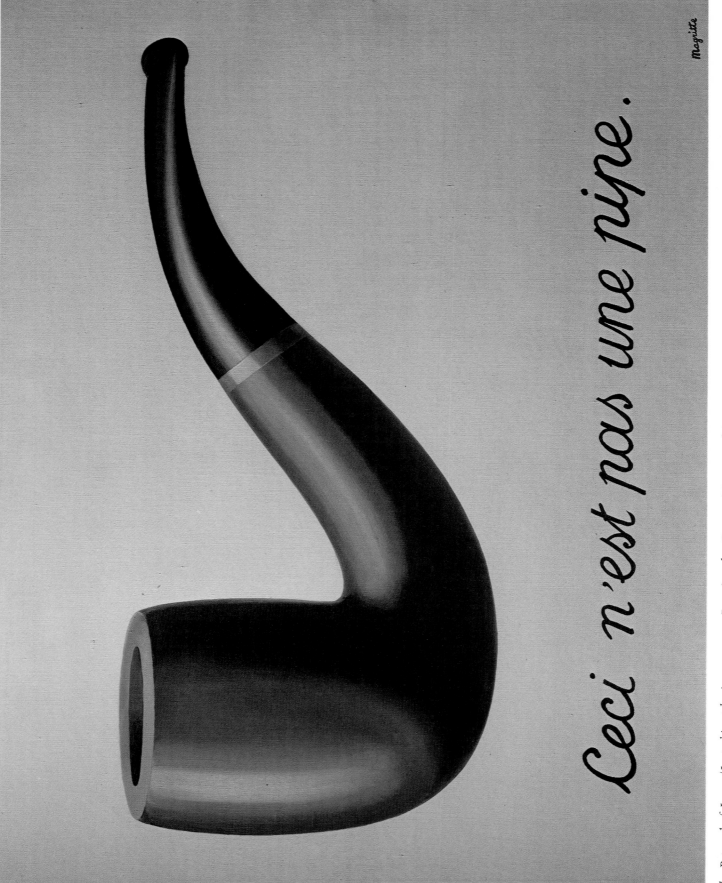

30. *The Betrayal of Images/La trahison des images.* 1929. Los Angeles County Museum of Art

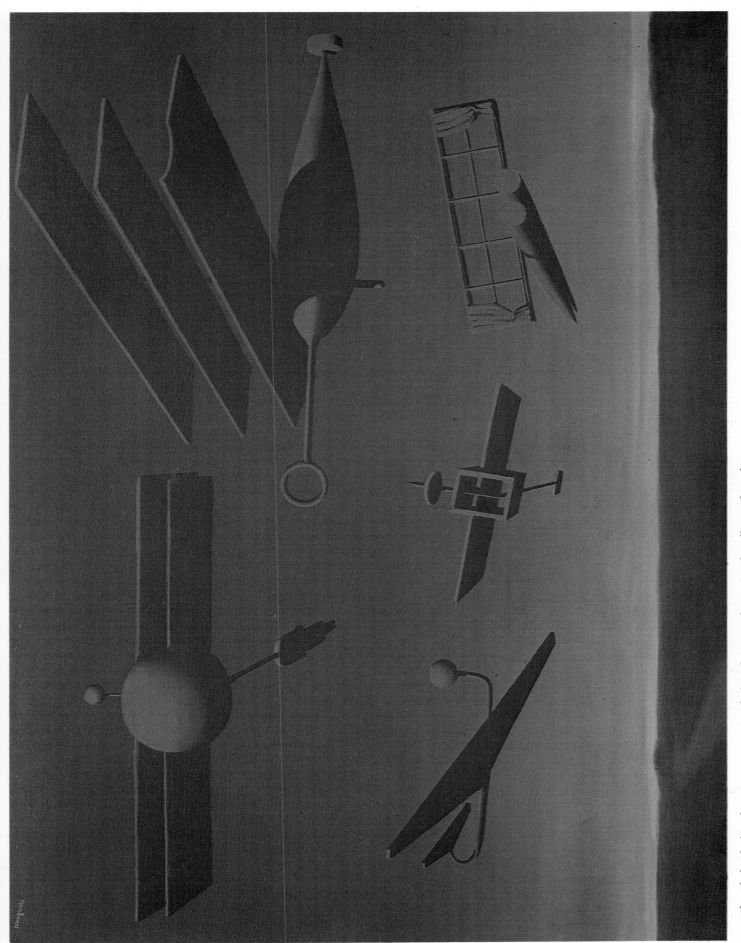

31. *The Black Flag*/*Le drapeau noir*. 1937. Edinburgh, Scottish National Gallery of Modern Art

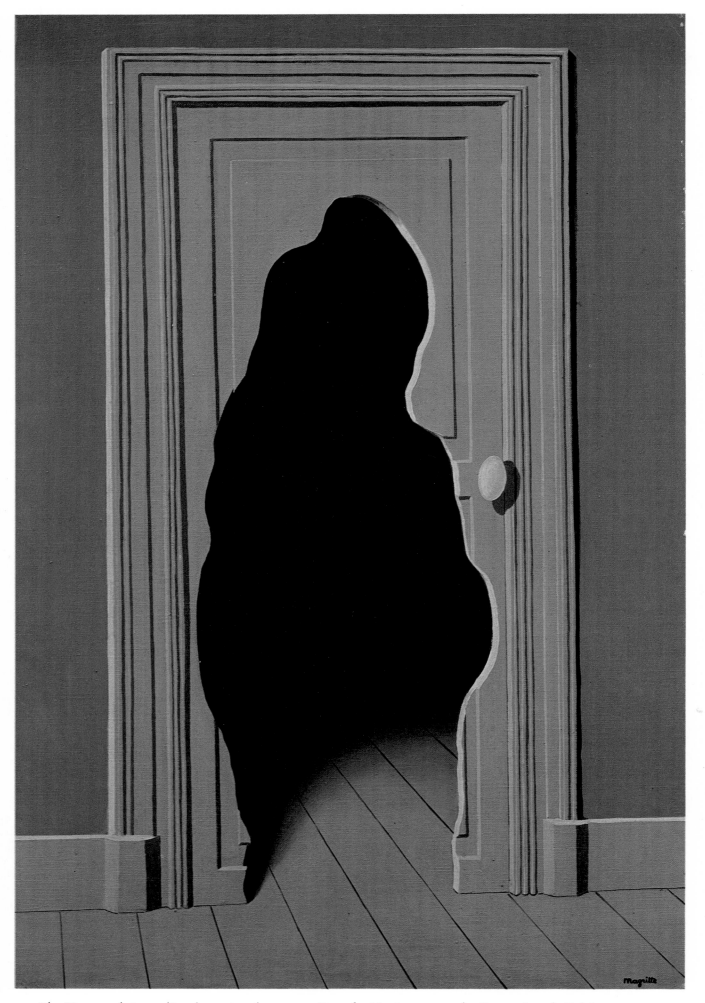

32. *The Unexpected Answer/La réponse imprévue.* 1933. Brussels, Musées royaux des Beaux-Arts de Belgique

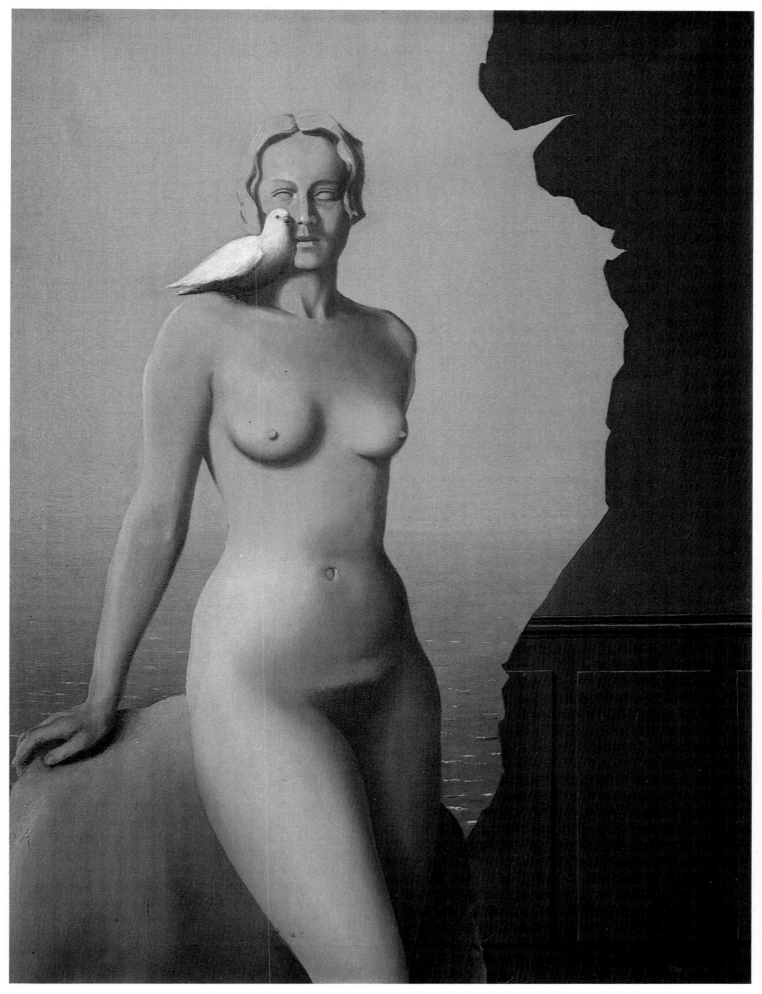

33. *Black Magic/La magie noire*. 1933 or 1934. Mme E. Happé-Lorge Collection

34. *The Human Condition/La condition humaine*. 1933. Private collection

35. *The Door to Freedom/La clef des champs.* 1936. Lugano-Castagnola, Switzerland, Thyssen-Bornemisza Collection

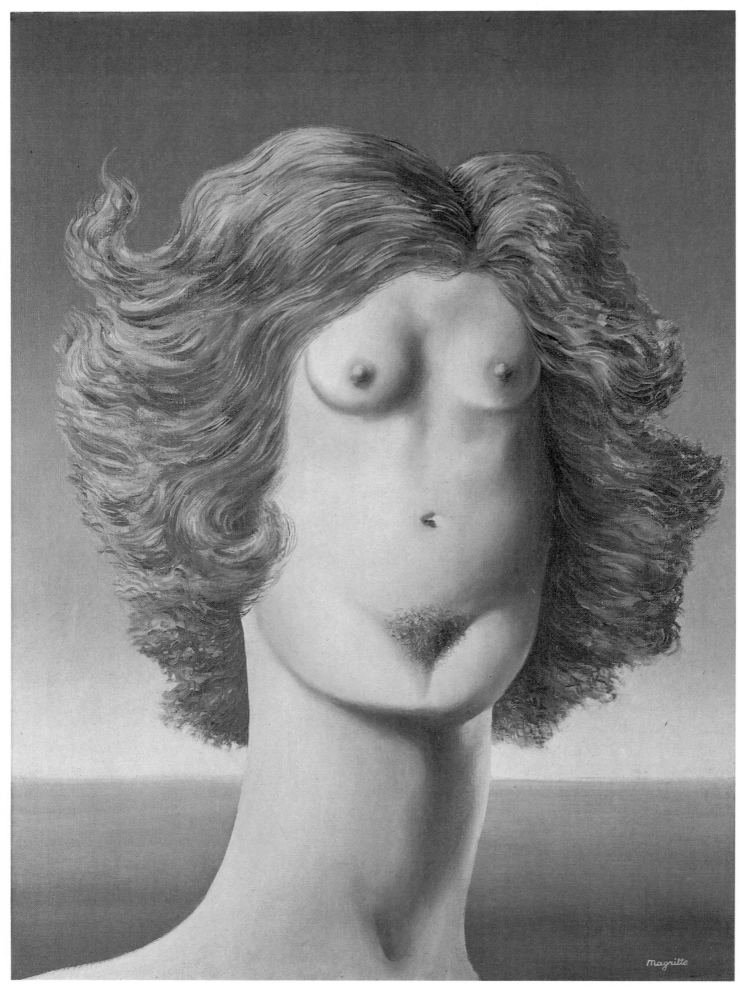

36. *The Rape/Le viol.* 1934. Houston, Menil Foundation Collection

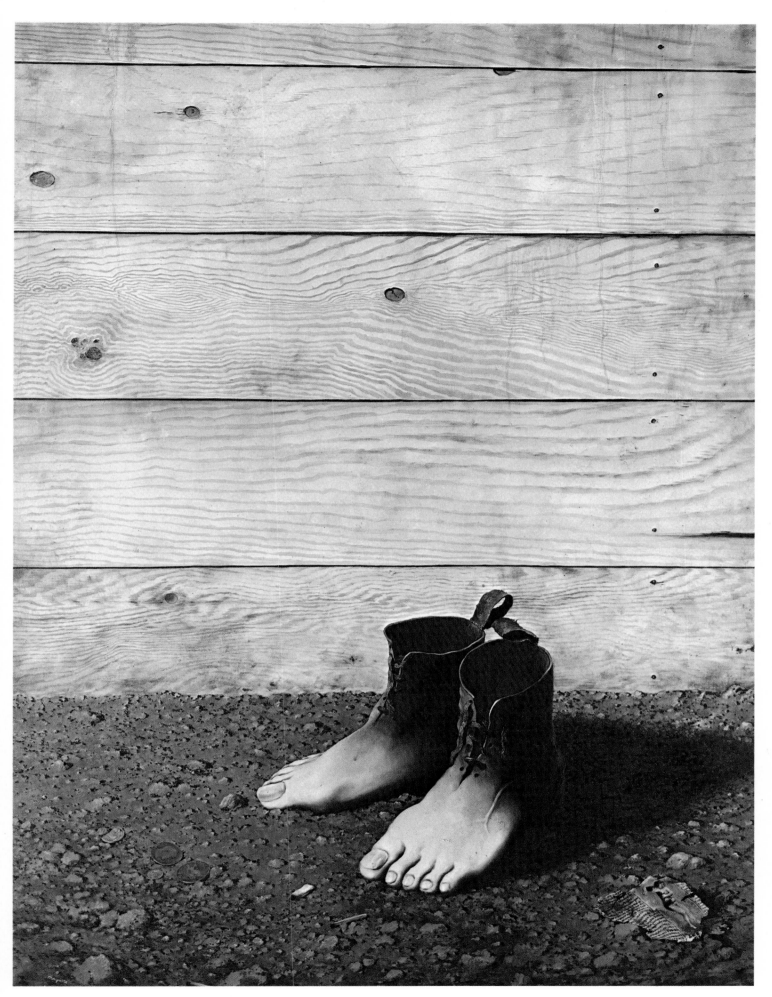

37. *The Red Model/Le modèle rouge.* About 1937. Sussex, Edward James Foundation (on loan to Brighton Art Gallery)

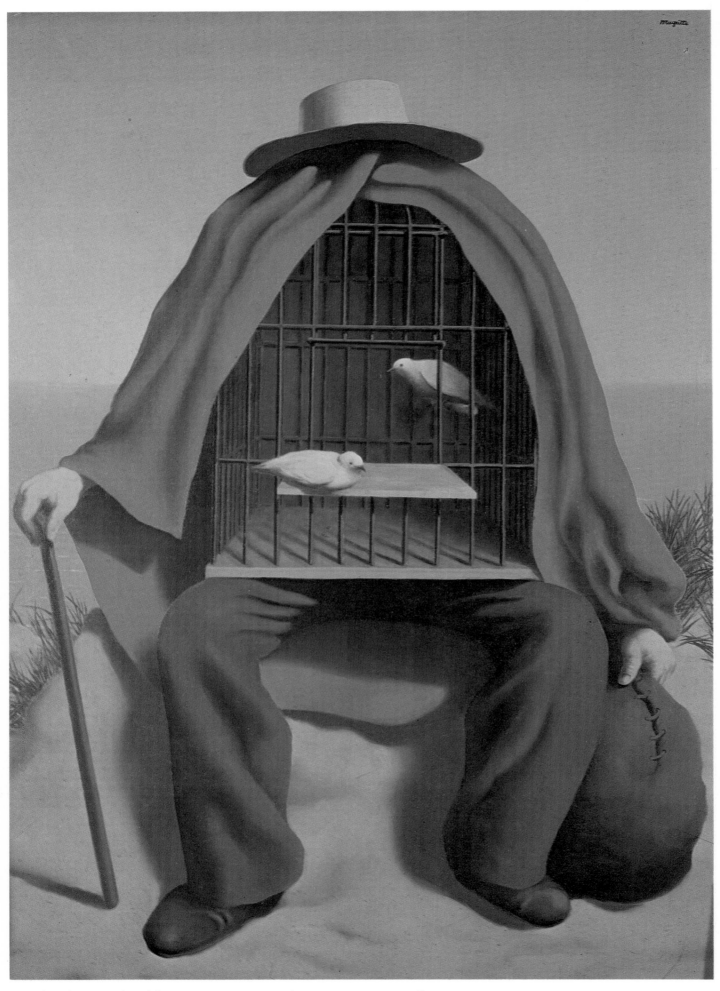

38. *The Therapeutist/Le thérapeute*. 1937. Baron and Baroness Urvater Collection

39. *Not to be Reproduced/La reproduction interdite.* 1937. Rotterdam, Museum Boymans – van Beuningen

40. *Time Transfixed/La durée poignardée*. 1939. Chicago, Art Institute

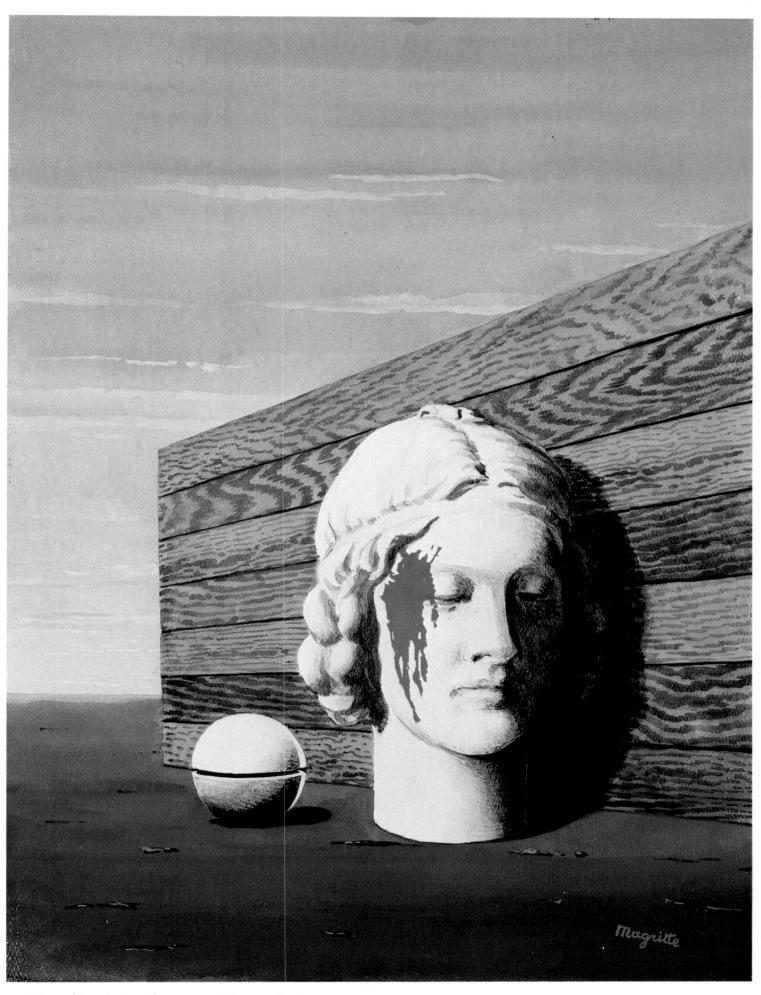

41. *Memory/La mémoire*. About 1942. Private collection

42. *The Ocean/L'océan*. 1943. Houston, private collection

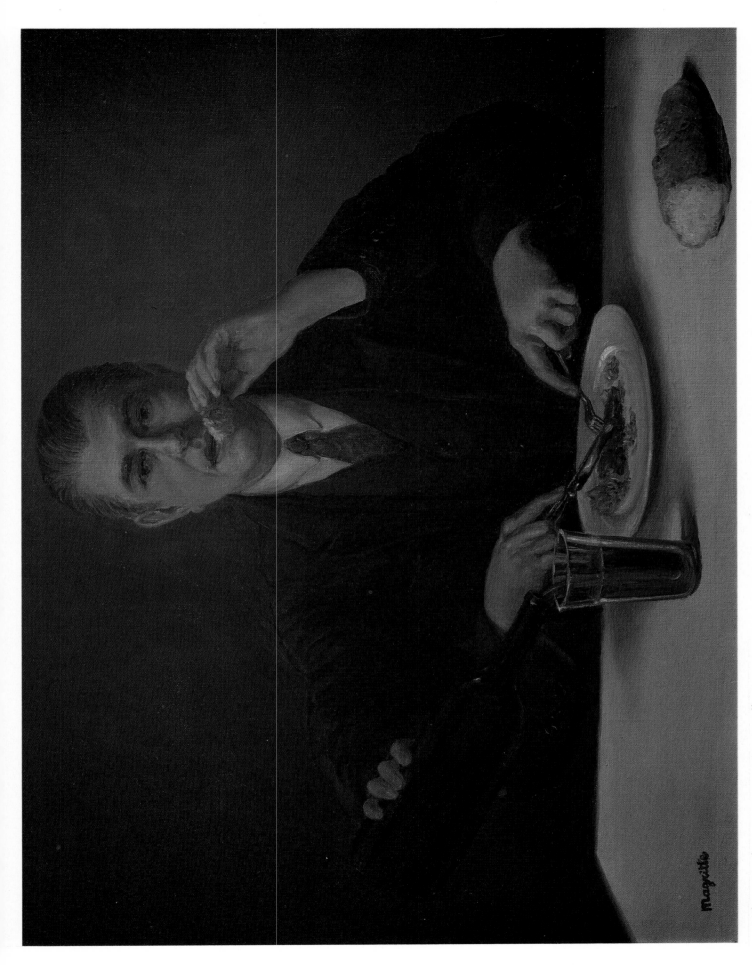

43. *The Sorcerer/Le sorcier.* 1951. Private collection

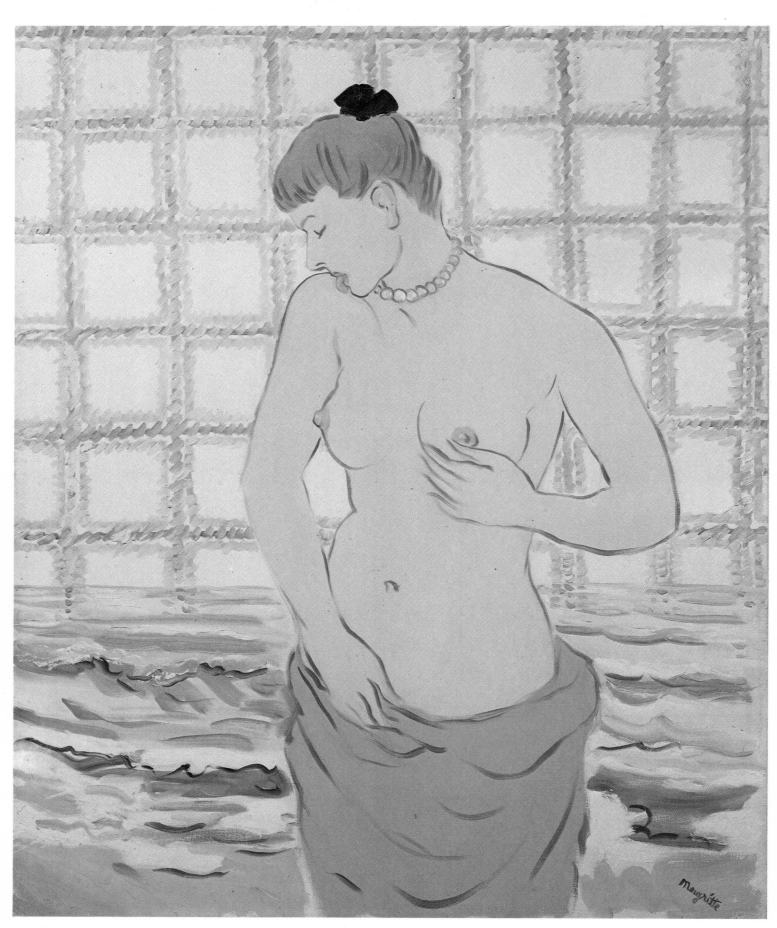

44. *The Pebble/Le galet.* 1948. Private collection

45. *The Song of the Violet*/*Le chant de la violette*. 1951. Private collection

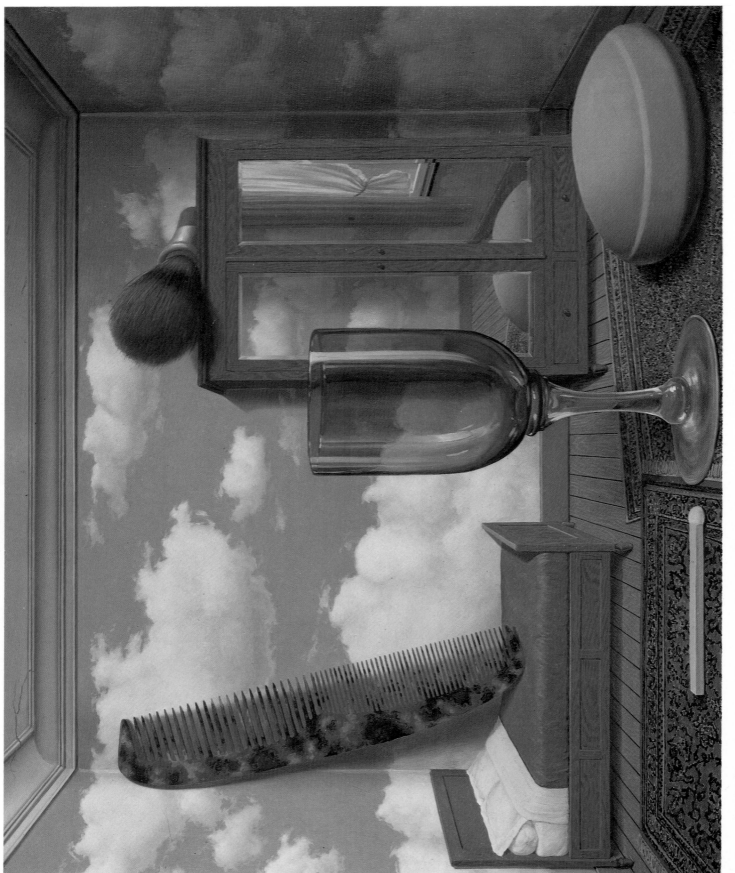

46. *Personal Values/Les valeurs personnelles*. 1951–2. Private collection

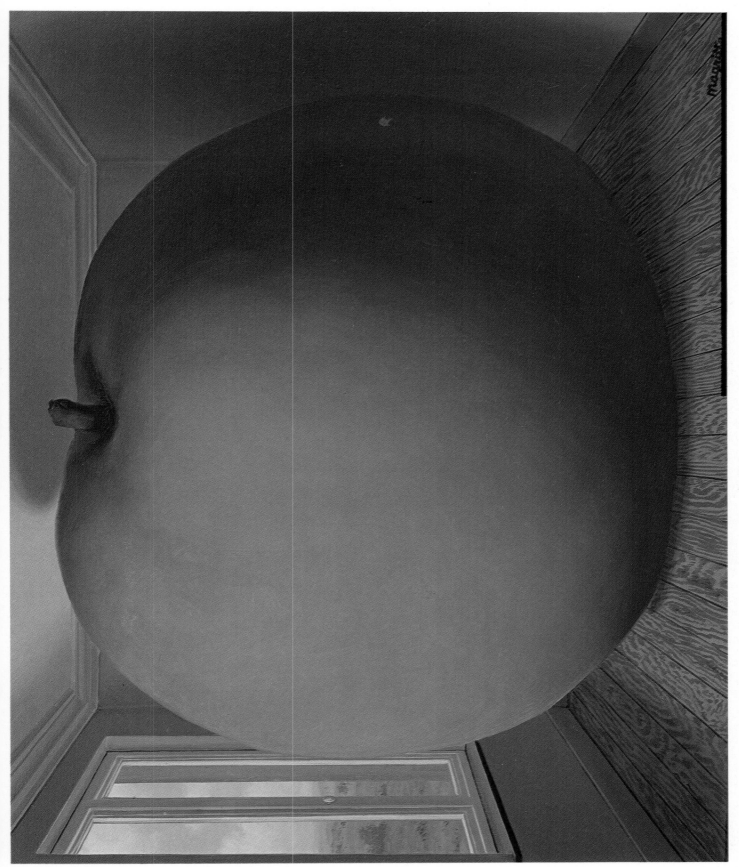

47. *The Listening Room/La chambre d'écoute.* 1952. U.S.A., private collection

48. *The Age of Enlightenment/Le siècle des lumières.* 1967. Private collection